ROTATION
PLAN

The Animal
Victoria Cross –
The Dickin Medal

The Animal Victoria Cross – The Dickin Medal

P.J. Hawthorne

Pen & Sword
MILITARY

First published in Great Britain in 2012 by
PEN & SWORD MILITARY
An imprint of
Pen & Sword Books Ltd
47 Church Street
Barnsley
South Yorkshire
S70 2AS

ISBN 978-1-78159-042-3

Typeset by Concept, Huddersfield, West Yorkshire
Printed and bound in England by CPI Group (UK) Ltd, Croydon, CR0 4YY.

Pen & Sword Books Ltd incorporates the imprints of Pen & Sword Aviation, Pen & Sword Family History, Pen & Sword Maritime, Pen & Sword Military, Pen & Sword Discovery, Wharncliffe Local History, Wharncliffe True Crime, Wharncliffe Transport, Pen & Sword Select, Pen & Sword Military Classics, Leo Cooper, The Praetorian Press, Remember When, Seaforth Publishing and Frontline Publishing.

For a complete list of Pen & Sword titles please contact
PEN & SWORD BOOKS LIMITED
47 Church Street, Barnsley, South Yorkshire, S70 2AS, England
E-mail: enquiries@pen-and-sword.co.uk
Website: www.pen-and-sword.co.uk

To Mum,

Sarah,

Toby (our cat)

and animal lovers everywhere ...

Contents

List of Plates

Acknowledgements

The first thank you is to Alison Doran who spent six months valiantly editing each story by working on two or three each week. The editing comments were invaluable but so too was the emotional reaction Alison would write at the bottom of each one, without her prompting I would not have sent the book to Pen & Sword. On one occasion Alison had a few minutes free before she was due to collect her daughters, Ellie and Myah, from school so began reading the three animals for the week. Unfortunately, Alison became so engrossed in the stories she was late collecting Ellie and Myah who, when she arrived at the school ten minutes late, were standing outside the school gates wet through due to rain. It was this type of comment and encouragement from Alison that gave me the confidence to approach a publisher.

Over the years many people gave their time and expertise generously to help me with the research of the subject. A particular thanks to Lesley Catton at my local library who, along with the other staff members (Mary Cooper, Fiona Hayward and Hayley Tranter), continually managed to locate books and articles at short notice and they never refused to help me despite being very busy! I would also like to thank Heather Bayne and Maureen Bozdech for their kind help and guidance. A particular thank you must also be mentioned to Claire Bennett whose relentless pursuit of the slightest clue on pigeons was priceless! The wise council and advice of Henry Wilson, John and Doreen Hughes, Chris Waters, Roger Hack and Julian and Jenny Maslin was invaluable.

Gill Hubbard, of the PDSA, in Telford provided some newspaper cuttings and press releases that were very useful and helped fire my interest in the Dickin Medal. From this small beginning I became fascinated by the subject and attempted to leave 'no stone unturned' when researching each animal.

Thanks also go to Lizzie Keen for her charming illustrations of the animals and Lisa Bialek, Richard Doughty, Rita O'Donoghue, Patricia O'Gorman and Stephanie Saville for their kind help with the photographs. Matt Jones, of the Pen & Sword production team, worked extremely hard to fine tune this book and it is much the better for it, I greatly appreciated his advice and support. The final thank you is for animal lovers everywhere, including you, for only an animal lover would buy such a book as this.

P.J. Hawthorne

Introduction

The Animal Victoria Cross, as it came to be called, was the brain-child of an animal lover called Maria Dickin. Its official name is The Dickin Medal and it is awarded to those animals who display outstanding loyalty, bravery and courage.

Maria Dickin was born in 1870 the eldest of eight children and grew to be by far the most determined. As the daughter of a Free Church Minister Maria had a comfortable childhood and married her first cousin, Arnold Dickin, a wealthy chartered accountant, in 1898, and settled down to domestic life in Hampstead Heath. As befitting the period, women of social standing were not expected to work but to look after the household. However, Maria was intelligent and bold and despite the social restrictions she set about helping others through a programme of social work in the East End of London visiting the sick and needy. Whilst walking through the grey, dank streets Maria was deeply affected by the sight of cats and dogs, sick and in appalling condition, fighting over the smallest scraps of food in gutters, often dragging behind lame or broken limbs. Many owners could not afford veterinary bills and animals often suffered slow, agonising deaths.

Maria resolved to do something and in 1917 set up the People's Dispensary for Sick Animals (PDSA) in a basement in Whitechapel with this sign outside:

> *Bring your sick animals.*
> *Do not let them suffer.*
> *All animals treated.*
> *All treatment free.*

Within hours the dispensary was overwhelmed with clients. Police were called to control the crowds of people and animals that flocked to the street above the basement. A few years later Maria converted a gypsy caravan into a horse-drawn mobile surgery, complete with trained veterinarian, in order to tour the East End to visit animals whose owners could not get to Whitechapel. The organisation began to spread across the nation and by 1923 there were sixteen dispensaries. Maria, with the support of the armed forces, started to expand into other countries in the British Empire to care for the animals. Tangiers, Palestine, South Africa, Greece and Egypt all had a PDSA programme treating animals injured in the line of duty when serving with the armed forces. Maria also helped to set up, in 1934, a Busy Bees programme that taught children how to care for their pets. Prior to the Second World War the PDSA had set up five hospitals, seventy-one dispensaries and had eleven motorised surgeries as well as a headquarters in Ilford, which provided veterinary training.

The outbreak of the Second World War brought great danger to many animals through army, naval and air force service, animals such as horses, mules and cattle were used to pull vehicles whilst homing pigeons were a vital means of communication. Others, as mascots, were taken abroad by the armed forces, some even went into battle. On the home front, through the death of their owners at the hands of enemy action, many pets were in danger of starving, particularly in the cities, which were regularly bombed by the *Luftwaffe* night after night.

Queen Victoria commissioned the creation of the Victoria Cross on 29 January 1856 after reading of heroic deeds in the Crimean War, to be awarded to servicemen for most conspicuous bravery, or some daring pre-eminent act of valour or self-sacrifice. Queen Victoria had been moved by acts of great bravery; so too was Maria. Prior to the Crimean War there was no award for the greatest acts of bravery by soldiers and animals have served in wars for centuries with no recognised reward. After the declaration of war in 1939 the War Office sent out a request for animals capable of helping the war effort. Many people struggled to feed themselves due to rationing and faced the heartbreak of releasing their pets. Thousands of horses, dogs, donkeys and pigeons were enlisted into the armed forces to perform a variety of roles. Some dogs acted as guards and others were able to detect buried victims of the blitz; some even went on secret missions with the SAS into enemy territory; all served with distinction.

In 1943, after reading of the bravery of these animals, Maria established the Dickin Medal, the highest award for animal bravery. This honour is recognised all over the world as the Animal Victoria Cross and is awarded for acts of immense courage. Since its inception the medal has only been awarded on sixty-three occasions to twenty-eight dogs, thirty-one pigeons, three horses and one cat. Each winner displayed great courage under difficult circumstances, some in peacetime and others during conflicts such as the Second World War, Palestine, Korea, the Yugoslav war, Iraq, Afghanistan and the war on Terror. By reading this book you can find out how Roselle, an American guide dog, saved her owner from the collapse of the twin towers on 9/11 or how Simon, a small black and white cat, helped rescue an entire ship's crew. Winners hail from all over the world and performed remarkable feats, such as G.I. Joe, an American pigeon, who managed to save the lives of approximately 1,000 soldiers in the Italian town of Colvi Vechia during the Second World War. The animals feature in conflicts on land, sea and in the air. The Irish pigeon, Paddy, used his secret weapon to travel faster on special missions and Gander, a Newfoundland dog from Canada, narrowly avoided being put to sleep but was smuggled out by soldiers to fight with distinction at the Battle of Lye Mun. Regal, a large bay gelding horse, won the Animal Victoria Cross for failing to react under the heavy blitz on London whilst Mercury managed to fulfil a dangerous mission for the resistance movement on the continent that eleven other pigeons failed to complete.

There are modern heroes too. Treo, a black Labrador saved countless lives in Afghanistan through his determination and skill whilst Sam, an Alsatian, helped prevent acts of ethnic cleansing during the Yugoslav war. There are also winners that were not enlisted in the armed forces. Sheila, a collie won her Dickin Medal whilst working as a sheepdog in the Cheviot Hills in Cumbria. Other animals completed such secret work that their owners were never told of their heroic deeds, other winners did not live to receive their medals.

Maria passed away in 1951 but lived to present some of the animals with their medals.

What follows are the stories of how each of the sixty-three animals won the Dickin Medal, I hope you gain as much pleasure from reading this book as I gained from writing it.

P.J. Hawthorne
October 2011

PART 1

WAR AT SEA

Beachcomber
Dieppe, 1942

On 17 August 1942, the clue 'French port (6)' appeared in the *Daily Telegraph* crossword. The solution printed the following day was 'Dieppe'. On 19 August, the Allied raid on Dieppe was scheduled to take place involving thousands of men, weapons and ships. Allied objectives included the control of a port on mainland Europe to prove that it could be done, to gather intelligence and destroy the German defences that faced the English Channel. British Intelligence immediately swung into action and set about trying to find out if the clue was a tip-off to the German Army that a raid was imminent.

The raid began at 05:00 hrs with over 6,000 infantrymen, predominantly Canadian, supported by large British naval and Allied air force contingents. Preparations had been made and a small pigeon by the name of Beachcomber had completed practice flights from Belfast, Berwick and Penzance to the loft in Reigate. Radio equipment was taken on the raid as communication between infantry, the Navy and Air Force was essential. Two pigeons were also included as a precaution. One of these birds was Beachcomber.

The raid did not start well. German defences were well positioned across the hills above the town. Their artillery fire was unerringly accurate raining down on the ships and vessels. The Germans moved toward the coast as if they had prior knowledge of the attack. Once on the beach, the Canadian men, with their equipment, were met by a barrage of machine gun fire from the seafront, which prevented them from making any progress into Dieppe itself. Radio communication with headquarters in England was broken and the men on the beach were pinned down by enemy gunfire. They could not withdraw as the ships and boats that had brought them across the Channel had turned back into open sea. In an act of desperation the two birds were released from the beach with details of the disastrous events. One of the birds was shot down by the German infantry almost immediately and fell into the sea. The only hope of rescue came from the second bird. This bird was Beachcomber.

Despite the shells and bullets whizzing past, Beachcomber managed to fly away from the battle zone and out to sea. Travelling at an average speed of over 50 mph, Beachcomber arrived at the operational headquarters with the messages still intact. The information presented to the operational command contributed to the decision to order a withdrawal at 09:00 hrs. None of the objectives had been completed and the raid was a disaster with over half the men involved killed, wounded or captured. The order for a withdrawal saved the remaining men from a battle that could not be won. Dieppe remained in German hands.

For completing a desperately important and dangerous flight in the face of huge odds, Beachcomber was awarded the Dickin Medal on 16 March 1944. The importance of this bird is underlined by the date of the award; the war was still raging and most creatures received their medals after hostilities had ended. Beachcomber's citation reads:

> *Beachcomber brought the first detailed news of the landing at Dieppe beach, with a second pigeon which was shot down. Beachcomber homed to Army Headquarters in the UK at over 50 mph.*

In the aftermath of such a disastrous attack on the German occupied mainland, the War Office suspected that the crossword had been used to pass intelligence to the enemy and called upon Lord Tweedsmuir, then a senior intelligence officer attached to the Canadian Army and MI5, to investigate. After an exhaustive inquiry, no evidence was found that could prove that the crossword had been used to tip off the enemy, it was simply regarded as a coincidence.

Simon
China, 1949

At the turn of the twentieth century, the Boxer Rebellion uprising took place in China in response to imperialist expansion involving European opium traders, political invasion and economic manipulation. The ruling Qing Dynasty was weakened by the rebellion and limped on to 1911 when it was overthrown. China had become a Republic. The Republic was very unstable as different factions fought each other for control of the country. Eventually, in 1927 a full scale war broke out between the Kuomintang (KMT or Chinese Nationalist Party), the governing party of the nation, and the Communist Party of China (CPC).

Under pressure from the advancing Communists, the Chinese Nationalist government moved from Nanking to Canton, but several of the European embassies remained in Nanking. After the end of the Second World War the British Ambassador decided to remain at his post, with the additional security of a Royal Naval battleship based in the city to protect the embassy and the numerous British nationals in the region. In 1949, HMS *Amethyst*, under the command of Captain Bernard Skinner, sailed to relieve the destroyer HMS *Consort* in Nanking. Built in Govan, the *Amethyst* was a modified frigate of the Black Swan Class built in 1943 and manned by a full crew, including a cat and a dog.

Simon, who was born on Stonecutter's Island near Hong Kong in 1946, was the ship's cat and 'mouser-in-chief'. He enjoyed wandering the ship visiting the crew and slept in the captain's quarters, despite the wishes of the captain himself. At dinner Simon would stroll across the guests' knees and could often be found sitting on charts on the bridge. There was also a terrier named Peggy with whom Simon would be friendly or, according to his whims, ignore. Both animals provided companionship for the crew and helped to boost morale, especially with long periods spent away from home on the high seas. On route to Nanking the ship anchored overnight at Kiangyin to collect supplies in Shanghai, before making its way toward Nanking.

Some days later, on 20 April in foggy weather, HMS *Amethyst* approached the mouth of the Yangtze River. The crew could not see anyone on the river bank. The north side of the Yangtze was patrolled by the Communist Army who had set up a base to monitor traffic on the river, but the ship was clearly marked with the Royal Navy flag flying from the mast. As the ship moved slowly up the river it was attacked, without warning, from the northern bank. A hail of bullets rained down on the crew. Some bullets caused a fire to break out onboard, which was swiftly dealt with, but worse was to come. The shore batteries started to bombard the ship with shells that went whizzing overhead or dropped short of the vessel sending water shooting into the air. Gradually, the shells began to find their target with direct hits on the *Amethyst* gouging gaping holes in the side of the ship, sending shrapnel spinning into the air, slicing everything in its path. Fires were reignited and the noise of the shells striking the ship was deafening. A direct hit on the open bridge killed the captain and seriously injured other officers including the second-in-command, Lieutenant Geoffrey Weston, who, despite being badly wounded, remained in command. The steel plate of the hull was pierced by a forceful explosion not 3 feet from Simon, creating a hole more than a foot. Suddenly, the barrage stopped and nothing could be heard amongst the night fog but the put-put-put of the ship's engine.

As a result of the damage to the bridge the ship drifted onto a sandbank and became beached. *Amethyst* had received fifty-four hits, the steering mechanism was jammed and seventeen men had been killed. Simon was badly injured; he was found unconscious with wounds to his back and left side and the fur around his face was singed, the crew picked him up and took him to the medical officer. The medic was also concerned about Simon's hearing after the deafening noise of the explosion; if he did regain consciousness there was a fear he would be 'bomb-happy' or shell shocked. Fearing Simon would not survive the night, the medical officer removed the shrapnel and stitched up his wounds, and made Simon as comfortable as possible. *Amethyst*, under the cover of night, moved off the sandbank and weighed anchor for fear of coming under attack again. News of the attack spread quickly across the world and people waited to see what would happen next. The Communists remained on the bank, heavily armed, whilst *Amethyst* did not move.

6

The crew had salvaged most of the food supply and distilled their own water. However, they were short of fuel due to a leak but they managed to patch up the damage. An attempt was made for a medical team to board *Amethyst* using a Sunderland Flying boat, but this craft was fired upon as soon as it landed on the river and was forced to retreat. Rats aboard the ship were breeding quickly and eating the food supply. This was a serious problem as no assistance could be given after the attack on the Sunderland craft and the Navy was keen to avoid provoking the Communists for fear of a further attack.

Diplomatic negotiations for the release of the vessel began and the British Embassy in Nanking decided to send Commander John Kerans, a military attaché, with replacement officers to assume command. It appeared that the crew was in for a long wait. The Chinese Nationalists guided Kerans to *Amethyst*, and once onboard, he organised the burial at sea for the seventeen men who had been killed. As soon as Kerans took control, Simon's condition improved and he began to roam the ship again.

Months passed with no movement and the summer months brought searing heat and biting mosquitoes, the ship's supply of food was running low and the Communists, keen to starve the men into surrender, would not allow fresh supplies to be taken aboard. Kerans cut rations in half but was also concerned about the rats aboard the ship which increased in numbers and continued to eat the crew's food. Simon was called into action and, despite his injuries, was put to work in the storage rooms below deck with the task of protecting the supplies and thus avoid surrender. Simon rose to this challenge magnificently and on his first day he caught a huge rat, he then began to catch so many that the crew registered them on a chart in the officers' mess. On average he caught a rat a day and the food remained safe. This boosted the morale of the crew and each 'kill' was celebrated. If Simon had refused to catch rats or allowed his wounds to prevent him working, the food stocks would have been seriously depleted and the men aboard would have been starved out. It was all the more important because the ship ran out of rat poison very quickly due to the sheer number of rats.

Despite the gallant efforts of Simon, Kerans knew that the situation could only get worse and he did not want to surrender to the

Communists. It was, however, 140 miles to the safety of international waters of which two thirds would be guarded by the Communists. On 30 July, Kerans decided to make a break for it. There would be no moon that night and he kept the plan to himself until mid-afternoon when he divulged details to his men, who were then instructed to go about their usual work to avoid arousing the suspicion of watching eyes from the shore. As darkness fell the nervous crew muffled the chain of the anchor and slowly raised it. Just as Kerans made the decision to sail, a steamer sailed up the river. This was the perfect cover for the escape and Kerans waited until the steamer drew level before giving the order to move off, using the noise of the steamer to camouflage *Amethyst*'s engines. The Chinese Communists did not suspect anything immediately but soon flares were fired into the air as they saw that *Amethyst* had sailed away.

A barrage of shells followed *Amethyst* as she increased speed but, miraculously, none hit their target. Kerans accelerated to top speed, hoping that swift movement down the Yangtze to the mouth of the river would surprise the Communists. For several hours *Amethyst* had a charmed life as she moved down river as she was not struck by a single shell. Upon reaching Woosung the ship was lit up by floodlight torches, but she was still not fired upon. *Amethyst* had made it to open waters and freedom. For Commander Kerans and the crew the relief was tremendous and every man survived the dash for safety, including Simon and Peggy. The ship sailed to Hong Kong for repairs and the crew recounted the story of their escape, whilst there Simon continued to catch a rat each day. The crew noted how Simon became aware of his importance, as on the return journey he would only use the Captain's quarters or the officers' mess.

In October, *Amethyst* sailed into Plymouth harbour and the story of their miraculous escape became worldwide news. Simon was the hero and was sent letters, telegrams as well as tins of cat food and money to buy cream. Lieutenant Weston received so many letters and gifts on Simon's behalf he organised an officer to look after 'cat affairs'. Commander Kerans recommended Simon for a Dickin Medal for saving the crew's food supply and continually boosting the morale of the men. The PDSA agreed and began to prepare an award ceremony, but Simon was held in quarantine in Surrey so was unable to take part.

The recommendation from Kerans read:

Simon, neuter cat, served on HMS Amethyst *during the Yangtze incident, disposing of many rats though wounded by shell blast. Throughout the incident his behaviour was of the highest order.*

Simon is the only feline to win the Dickin medal and it was the first time an animal belonging to the Royal Navy won the award.

Sadly, when vets examined Simon in quarantine they discovered that, despite being only four years old, the stress of the Yangtze incident had left him with a weak heart and an infection (acute gastritis). Simon died on 28 November 1948; he was buried in the PDSA cemetery in Ilford. In a coffin lined with cotton wool and with a Union Jack draped over the top, Simon's corpse was lowered reverently into his grave, surrounded by dozens of bouquets of flowers sent from all over the country. The crew was saddened by his death as Simon had done so much to help them through the crisis on the Yangtze.

Winkie

The North Sea, 1942

This pigeon was a blue chequered hen, bred by Mr A.R. Colley, trained by the National Pigeon Service and given the code NEHU.40.NS.1. On 23 February 1942 a Beaufort RAF Bomber was returning from a flight to Norway to its base at RAF Leuchars in Fife with the pigeon on board. The Beaufort had been damaged and was limping across the North Sea, edging closer to the icy waves below. The crew attempted radio contact with their base and did make temporary contact, but the signal was too weak for the headquarters to locate their final position.

As the Beaufort plunged into the sea, a wing detached from the main body and the fuselage split open. Icy water gushed into the plane and the crew were thrown into the sea. Pigeons were held in steel containers that were dislodged from the inside of the plane and NEHU.40.NS.1 was catapulted into the oily water. The crew managed to find a rubber dinghy and climbed in, only to discover that they were over 100 miles from the base at Leuchars. One of the crew, amongst the fire and noise, spotted a pigeon fighting to get airborne despite the oily water that matted her plumage. The men paddled to her and picked her up out of the sea.

Meanwhile, at RAF Leuchars, an air search was immediately launched after the failed radio contact, but with choppy waters and an approximate search area of 70 square miles of sea, hopes of rescue were not high. The men in the dinghy had only one chance and began to wipe the oil from the bird's feathers while a message was prepared:

Distance to base 129 miles, nearest land 120 miles, 1½ hours of daylight left.

The crew knew that if she did not make it to Leuchars they would not survive for long in such conditions. The bird was thrust into the air, struggled to force herself upwards from the oily water but eventually circled the wreckage and flew off, albeit slowly. A pigeon usually uses the sun to gauge a flight path and in such weather conditions, with poor visibility, the chances of getting through to her loft were small, and would be even smaller when she could not fly as efficiently as usual due to the hindrance from the oil matting her feathers.

At 08:20 hrs the next day, the oil-stained bird arrived at her loft clearly suffering from stress and exhaustion and with one eyelid blinking rapidly, a sign of considerable strain and stress. Sergeant Davidson of the Pigeon Service examined her and tried to clean off the remaining oil. Unfortunately she was not carrying her message. However, Davidson noted her code name NEHU.40.NS.1 and realised immediately which plane she was from. Judging from the condition of the pigeon, the distance she could cover in her state, the last radio contact with the crew and the weather conditions, Sergeant Davidson knew the area being searched had to be re-directed. Fifteen minutes after taking off, a crew of the Royal Netherlands Air Service in a Hudson aircraft located the stricken crew.

Upon returning to RAF Leuchars, the crew decided to hold a banquet in honour of the pigeon and her trainer, who had saved their lives. The crew were joined by NEHU.40.NS.1, who was given a large wicker basket in which to perch, and the men decided that the pigeon deserved a proper name, as at this point the pigeon was known simply by her code. Due to the effort and exertion of her flight, this remarkable pigeon for the rest of her life was left with a constant blinking in one eye. The men therefore named her 'Winkie'.

The Flying Dutchman
Occupied Europe, 1944

The Flying Dutchman refers to a seventeenth-century nautical folk tale of a ghost ship forever destined to sail the high seas. Laden with treasure following a horrible act of murder or mutiny the ship became a ghost vessel. It was left to constantly sail the high seas and sightings have been claimed right into the twentieth century, as the crew supposedly attempt to make contact with living sailors to pass on messages to landlubbers or people long dead.

One of the most trusted pigeons during the war in Europe was a dark-chequered cock bird given the code NPS.42.NS.44802. During 1942 and 1943 he was assigned to light aircraft in the North Sea, and on many occasions he completed flights from crash-landed light aircraft. After proving himself he was selected for the most dangerous work: accompanying agents dropped behind enemy lines on the continent. On three occasions he homed in with important messages in March, May and June 1944, each time covering a distance of between 150 and 250 miles in good time. In fact, he frequently managed to return with the messages on the same day he was released.

On a fourth mission, in August 1944, he was released by his agent with a message but sadly never returned home to his loft. The Flying Dutchman ghost ship could never make port; NPS.42.NS.44802 was named after the ship as he was assumed lost at sea, never to return home.

White Vision
Scotland, 1943

White Vision was a white hen pigeon bred by the Fleming Brothers in Motherwell and based in Scotland. RAF duties in Scotland included searching for and attacking U-boats returning to Germany or Norway; flying boats operated from the Shetland Islands completing twenty-two hour shifts. Each crew was provided with two carrier pigeons should radio contact fail whilst on a mission.

Towards the end of one flight in October 1942, the weather turned foggy with high winds. The crew of a Catalina aircraft were denied permission to land at Sullom Voe in the Shetlands and redirected to Aberdeen. Upon reaching Aberdeen the weather was just as poor and they were redirected, yet again, to Oban. With fuel running low tension in the cockpit mounted. At 08:20 hrs the Catalina ran out of petrol and a crash landing was forced upon the pilot. The plane ditched into the water just off the Hebrides. The sea was cold and extremely violent as the crew crawled out of the plane and onto the wings. As they did so the radio operator made one last attempt to contact headquarters in the Shetlands to inform them of their position and request a rescue attempt. Radio contact failed but the two pigeons had been collected as the men clambered out onto the wings.

Two of the airmen then got into one of the life rafts, which was immediately carried away by the strong currents, leaving nine men with one life raft that would not take their combined weight in such weather conditions. Rather than draw lots for the relative safety of the dinghy, each man voted to release the pigeons and stay with the stricken plane that was slowly sinking into the icy sea.

With eleven lives at stake the two pigeons were released with the message:

Aircraft ditched safely NW Hebrides ... Heavy swell, taxying SE. No Casualties.

The pigeons were faced with 25 mph headwinds and an approximate visibility of 100 yards. The fog meant the sun could not be seen and this was the optimum tool of the pigeon to reach 'home' in their lofts in the Shetlands. One pigeon was never seen again.

White Vision, however, arrived at her loft at 5.00 pm the same day having covered a distance of over 60 miles in terrible conditions with a visibility of only 300 yards when she arrived. White Vision landed in a state of exhaustion and with a number of feathers missing but with the message intact. An air sea rescue attempt was launched as the scale of the search could be concentrated in one area.

After forty hours the search party had still not located the stricken Catalina. The plane was submerged beneath the icy waves with only one wing visible above the water with all nine men still clinging on for safety. The two men in the dinghy had not been seen since drifting away the previous day. At 12:05 hrs a rescue plane circled above and landed next to the Catalina. It was just in time; the plane sank minutes after the last airman stepped from it and onto the rescue plane.

The two men who were swept away in the other life raft were picked up later the same day and all eleven men owed their lives to a pigeon who did not give up despite appalling weather conditions. White Vision was awarded the Dickin Medal for saving those lives, the citation reads:

For delivering a message under exceptionally difficult conditions and so contributing to the rescue of an Air Crew while serving with the RAF in October 1943.

DD43T139

New Guinea, 1945

In July 1945 the American cargo ship *1402* moved through the waters near Madang off the coast of New Guinea. Aboard were vital supplies of ammunition, food and medical equipment due to be delivered to servicemen fighting the Japanese. Also on board was a blue cock pigeon who belonged to the Australian Voluntary Pigeon Service. This bird was very special and carefully selected to accompany the cargo ship on its vital journey. Trained by a Mr Adams in Victoria, Australia, the pigeon had previously completed twenty-three successful operational flights covering a total of 1,000 miles unscathed and had therefore been chosen from the 1st Australian Pigeon Service.

During an exceptionally heavy tropical storm the cargo ship lost its way and crashed onto Wadou Beach, on the Huon Gulf, became stuck in thick sand and was unable to move. The hull was damaged and sand and water flooded in. The engine broke down and radio contact with headquarters in Madang could not be established. This was an extremely serious predicament both for the men on board and those on shore relying on supplies being delivered. If a Japanese ship or foot patrol were to see the ship, those aboard would either be killed or taken prisoner. The men were 40 miles from their base at Madang. The captain had little room for manoeuvre and decided to release the bird immediately with the following message:

To: Detachment 55 Australian Port Craft Company, MADANG. From AB 1402. Date 12.7.45. Engine failed. Wash on to beach at WADAU owing very heavy seas. Send help immediately. Am rapidly filling with sand. TOO: 0800 – Sender's signature – HOLLAND Cpl. TO Liberation 0805 – No. of copies 2. TOR at Loft – 0855.

Hopes for the bird, despite its excellent record, were not high due to the storm that was raging overhead. Heavy rain and high winds that had caused the ship to crash would surely make the journey of 40 miles to the pigeon loft at Madang extremely difficult. The men on the ship prepared themselves for a possible attack from a Japanese patrol or a ship and attempted to move the cargo to protect it from the sand and water seeping into the hull.

15

Astonishingly, the bird covered the distance in atrocious weather in just fifty minutes. A ship was immediately dispatched to save the men and the cargo aboard *1402*. The men were rescued and the vital cargo retrieved. Not only that, *1402* was towed back to Madang and salvaged.

For making the journey in adverse weather conditions, saving the life of an entire crew as well as a ship and its cargo, DD43T139 was awarded the Dickin Medal by the Reverend West in St Dunstans-in-the-East on 26 February 1947. The inscription on the medal reads:

Awarded to pigeon DD43T139 for gallantry carrying a message through a severe tropical storm thereby bringing help to an army boat with vital cargo, in danger of floundering.

Tyke (*aka* Georgie)
The Mediterranean, 1943

Born in Cairo, Tyke was trained by the Middle East Pigeon Service and is the second Egyptian winner of the Dickin Medal after Tich, the black mongrel dog. Recognised for his speed and determination, Tyke was selected to accompany an American Air Force bombing operation across North Africa in June 1943. The plane suffered mechanical problems and the pilot quickly realised they would not reach their Mediterranean base. Another problem was the weather. It was a foggy day with heavy rain and visibility was extremely poor, at most 2 miles. The pilot searched for a safe place to land. Faced with a crash-landing in such conditions and in enemy-held territory, the pilot decided to ditch the plane into the Mediterranean and hope for air rescue.

As the plane drifted lower and lower, the crew of four radioed an SOS message that was recognised by the airbase but the only information about location transmitted was '100 miles off the coast'. After a successful crash landing each man escaped into a dinghy. To make matters worse, Tyke was removed from his cage and released into the air without a complete message. It read:

Crew safe in dingy 10 west of

The men were in a perilous position. Tyke was faced with a flight of 100 miles in awful conditions whilst the crew struggled to keep afloat in stormy waters. An air search was started immediately but with visibility so poor the attempt was unsuccessful and the aircraft had to return to base. On arrival they learned that, despite the weather, Tyke had homed in with his incomplete message.

Calculating the average speed of Tyke's flight and accounting for the weather, a search was begun and the entire crew was picked up safe and well from their dingy. Upon reaching the safety of base, the crew thanked Tyke for saving their lives and the pigeon received the Dickin Medal for courage after completing a flight under adverse conditions that led to the rescue of four airmen. The citation reads:

For delivering a message under exceptionally difficult conditions and so contributing to the rescue of an Air Crew, while serving with the RAF in the Mediterreanean in June, 1943.

Dutch Coast
Holland, 1942

On the night of 12/13 April 1942, a bombing sortie was making its way back to Britain after attacking strategic targets on mainland Europe. As was often the case, one bomber had been damaged by enemy action and began losing height rapidly whilst travelling over Holland. The pilot was forced to ditch the craft in the North Sea just off the Dutch coast, which was patrolled by German U-boats. At 6.00 am the crew bailed out of the stricken plane and floated in a dinghy, pondering their options.

The crew could not hope to paddle their way home to the English coastline (the sea was rough with a strong wind) and they had no wish to give themselves up to the Germans in occupied Holland. Before evacuating the sinking bomber the crew managed to collect NURP 41.A.2164, a pigeon held in a cage. The crew swiftly released the bird with a message of their whereabouts at 06:20 hrs, hoping for rescue, and began to move the dinghy away from the Dutch coastline to avoid being spotted as the daylight became brighter.

NURP.41.A.2164 'homed' in at 13:50 hrs the same day, having covered a distance of 288 miles in seven-and-a-half hours in adverse weather, carrying a message explaining the crash and the location of the crew. An aircraft was despatched immediately to rescue the men. This flight was the best performance by a pigeon in the National Pigeon Service at the time and the bird, newly named 'Dutch Coast' for the part played in rescuing the crew, was immediately awarded the Dickin Medal for such an outstanding flight.

Rifleman Khan
Holland, 1944

On 25 July 1947, the 6th Battalion of the Cameroonian Regiment paraded through Lanark in honour of a man and his dog who had been awarded the freedom of the Burgh. The war had ended two years previously and the regiment had served in almost every battle zone during the conflict. The regiment was founded in 1689 as the Scottish Rifles and had a long tradition. The man leading the parade was Corporal Muldoon and the dog became known as Rifleman Khan.

Khan was an Alsatian who belonged to a family named Railton living at Tolworth in Surrey and was a favourite playmate of Barry, their youngest son. As a puppy Khan had always displayed great intelligence and an eagerness to learn and was handed to the War Office when the request for dogs was announced and then sent to the War Dogs Training School. It was here that Khan excelled; he completed the course within six weeks, after which he was attached to the Cameroonians together with his handler, Corporal Muldoon. They were called into action on 2 November 1944 as part of an infantry mission to seize the Dutch island of Walcheren.

The Cameroonians were part of a twofold plan. The first part was to control the port of Flushing from which the entrenched Germans could see across the expanse of water, the Sloe Channel, leading into Antwerp. Nothing could sail down the river without being noticed. The second part of the mission was to take the island of Walcheren, which was only separated from the mainland by a canal.

The plan did not work. The heavy precision bombing from Lancasters did not soften up the German forces, despite approximately 1,200 tonnes of high explosives being dropped. The initial advances by infantry divisions had met with heavy losses and casualties. A new plan was devised but was inherently dangerous as it meant a direct infantry assault after crossing the Sloe Channel without the protection of any natural cover. The men would also have to tackle a mile-long stretch of mud-bank.

The night of 2 November proved dark and cold. At 03:30 hrs the men of the Cameroonians clambered aboard a flotilla of small boats in preparation for the assault. Rifleman Khan sat between

Muldoon's legs. As they entered the Sloe it was not long before the boats were spotted and a hail of shells greeted them, smashing into the water and covering the boats in spray. Machine gun fire rang out across the channel and the bullets raked the cold waves as the boats swayed from side to side trying to avoid the searchlights panning the sea. Each boat became a sitting duck, but the vessel carrying Rifleman Khan and Muldoon edged closer to the muddy bank. They were nearly there when a loud explosion was heard. They were thrown up into the air. Rifleman Khan crashed down into the cold water and he began paddling frantically to keep afloat, he managed to dodge the shells and machine gun fire to reach the muddy shore.

Instantly his paws sank into the heavy mud and around him Cameroonians were also waist deep. Their heavy weapons and equipment sent them plunging quickly into the mud. Rifleman Khan struggled through the ooze and sped up to higher ground. Below he saw the battle in full rage; men were drowning and others were struggling in the mud to reach the shore. Shells and bullets rained down on the Channel. However, Rifleman Khan was searching only for Muldoon. Over the noise of combat below – men screaming or shouting orders, bullets and shells being fired and boats creaking as they sank into the Sloe – Rifleman Khan heard the familiar shout of Corporal Muldoon.

On impact Muldoon had also been thrown into the cold, muddy water, but he could not swim and was stuck in the thick sediment, struggling to keep his head above water. Twice he had gulped muddy water whilst screaming for help but no-one could reach him. Rifleman Khan did not hesitate. Upon hearing the desperate cries of his handler he dashed back toward the Sloe and fought his way through the thick mud and water. As he approached, Muldoon's head was barely above the waves washing onto the beach but Khan did not hesitate. He managed to reach his handler, clamped his teeth around the collar of his tunic and gave a sharp tug. Muldoon remained stuck in the mud. Rifleman Khan tugged again and slowly but surely managed to pull him free.

Muldoon held on as Rifleman Khan paddled toward the shore. Still enemy gunfire pierced the water around them but neither was hit and they collapsed exhausted onto the beach. Muldoon coughed up water and mud but Rifleman Khan, after shaking off the water from his coat, began pulling him to firmer ground. However, when they reached a bank Muldoon watched as his dog collapsed exhausted onto the ground gasping for air. Many men of the Cameroonians lost their lives in the assault, Muldoon would have been one of those were it not for the bravery of Rifleman Khan whose Dickin Medal recommendation came four months later.

The citation reads:

> *For rescuing Lance Corporal Muldoon from drowning under heavy shellfire at the assault of Walcheren, November 1944 while serving with the 6th Cameroonians.*

Lance Corporal Muldoon and Rifleman Khan both survived the war, in 1946 the former returned to his work as a slater and plasterer in Strathaven, Scotland. He wrote many letters to the War Office requesting permission to keep Rifleman Khan permanently. Each request was rejected as the Railton family wanted their dog back. During the war years their son Barry had contracted infantile paralysis (polio) and wanted Rifleman Khan to return home.

In July 1947 Rifleman Khan was invited to the National Dog Tournament at Wembley Stadium, which prompted Mr Railton to write to Muldoon and ask if he would like to lead the family dog around the parade ring on the day. The former Lance Corporal jumped at the chance. When the two met Mr Railton was so touched by their affection for each other that he shook the hand of Muldoon and said, 'He's yours.'

Navy Blue
France, 1944

For delivering an important message from a raiding party on the west coast of France although injured, while serving with the RAF in June 1944

This RAF-trained pigeon had an excellent flying record for the Air/Sea Rescue during the war and was given the name 'Navy Blue' as well as the code NPS.41.NS2862. As a fast and reliable bird Navy Blue was selected for a special mission accompanying a small reconnaissance party on the west coast of France in 1944. Landing via sea, the party would move inland to complete an observation mission and use Navy Blue to carry the information back to Plymouth, a distance of over 200 miles.

On 15 June 1944 Navy Blue was issued to the men, but due to bad weather in the Channel, the mission was delayed until the night of 17 June. The men landed after midnight on the morning of the 18th and carried out their objective. Navy Blue was released by the men, however she was almost immediately attacked by a predator and badly injured. Navy Blue did not give up and managed to continue flying, reaching her loft at Plymouth at 02:45 hrs on 19 June.

The message was of immense value to the Intelligence Branch. Owing to her determination to deliver the message, despite terrible injuries, Navy Blue was awarded the Dickin Medal. Thankfully this brave pigeon recovered from her injuries in time to accept the award in March 1945.

PART 2

THE HOME FRONT

Rex

London, 1945

Rex, an Alsatian, was one of fourteen dogs employed during the war to find people buried under their houses and other debris during the attacks on London. In January 1945, before his training was complete, he was thrust into action in Lambeth when a bombing raid destroyed a row of houses. Whilst being led through the debris over a track cleared through the rubble Rex began to show the signs indicating that someone was buried. Having not completed his training and digging on a path that had been followed before and was well worn, the rescue team moved Rex away from the path to another area of the bomb site.

However, the men saw Rex was clearly agitated when pulled away and began scratching violently at the soft earth. They joined in the digging and a matter of inches from the surface they discovered the earth was saturated with warm blood. Further excavations unearthed a collapsed wall, which also had blood on it, but upon removing the bricks one by one they could see nothing to indicate a trapped person. Rex had been rested whilst the bricks were removed, but he was soon brought back to the site and again began to dig away through earth and debris. The rescue team again joined in and together they discovered the corner of a mattress, which Rex began to tear at with his teeth. The rescue team frantically pulled bricks and mortar away to reveal two people, who, sadly, had already died from their injuries. They were still in their pyjamas underneath the bed clothes.

In March 1945 Rex, along with other rescue dogs, was sent to the site of a still-burning factory that had been wrecked by a Doodlebug. The greatest fear for dogs and many other animals is fire; Rex was initially instructed to scour the section of the wrecked building that was not burning. This he did and gave indication to the rescue team of several sites that were quickly cleared and rescues completed. Rex was then instructed to do the same in the part that was still burning but the signal to remove him was given after the remaining walls and floors began to tumble to the ground. Rex refused to leave the site and had to be dragged away by his collar in an agitated state. This bravery is remarkable, his only instinct was for those people buried or endangered and his actions were completely selfless.

Later in the day he was recalled to the factory as the fire had been brought under control and largely extinguished but fire crews continued to spray water across the debris as it was very hot and the dogs could not remain on the hot ground for long periods. Despite this heat, Rex made his way across the debris and gave an indication of five casualties within four minutes of returning to the site, a remarkable feat given the conditions. The bodies were recovered within fifteen minutes of Rex returning to the factory.

Two days later, Rex was brought back to the site after the ground had cooled and all the fires were extinguished. Rex arrived after working at another site and was suffering the effects of a gas leak. He was vomiting and clearly unwell. On arrival he overcame this and methodically examined the ground but was withdrawn by his handler under protest.

One of the final assignments Rex completed during the war involved a collapsed block of flats at Stepney where the damage was considerable. Upon being released he immediately ran to a partially remaining stairwell and was instantly removed by his handler, as this was not the site he had been brought to examine. Once he was unleashed on the debris of some flats where casualties were suspected, he did not even start work and simply ran off to the stairwell. The rescue team followed, began digging and found several bodies.

This remarkable animal continued to display the same determination and single-mindedness in peacetime. Rex was called into action in 1947 when the William Pit collapsed at Whitehaven, Cumbria. On 15 August 1947 at 17:40 hrs there was an explosion in the mine; firedamp propagated by coal dust, with ignition caused by shot firing in waste. The first bulletin with details of the accident was issued by Mr J.G. Helps, the National Coal Board Area General Manager, who was in charge of the rescue operation. It was thought that 121 men (a figure later altered to 117) were in the pit at the time. Of these, three men had come out of the pit and seven others were known to be safe. In total 104 lives were lost but six of the bodies had not been discovered. On 19 August Rex, along with another Dickin Medal winner Jet, were set a training exercise to see if they were up to the job of entering the mine. The dogs passed with flying colours, unearthing a man buried underneath debris. Both animals were sent into the William Pit mine to locate remains buried under loose and fallen rock, which was dangerous work. The remaining six bodies were recovered.

Rex is unique because he had not completed his training when he first went into action and displayed his talent and skill when others had not realised people were buried under so much debris. Each animal in wartime service had a report compiled on the quality of work. Rex's report states:

There can be no question that he fully understands what is expected of him and he shows determination in exploration, which has so often produced results. On occasions his searches have led him through smouldering debris, thick smoke, and heat. He has ignored fire hoses spraying quantities of water around him, and has not hesitated to climb over loose and dangerous rubble in his efforts to follow up a scent, which may have led to a trapped casualty. He has very often given clear indications of the exact whereabouts of missing persons, thereby enabling rescue or search work to be carried out at those precise places, saving an enormous amount of time and labour in the clearing up of the incidents.

Upstart
London, 1944

At Hyde Park, during the Second World War, anti aircraft batteries were stationed to defend London against the Blitz. As the city came under attack night after night the guns would fire until they were red hot. Next to the batteries a stable was established for the horses of the London Police. Each time the guns fired the animals were fed to keep them calm. One horse in the stable, named Upstart, would win the Dickin Medal.

One night the stables received a direct hit, Upstart did not panic and stood calmly until he was rescued from the smoke and noise; no doubt expecting to be fed. Upstart was relocated to a new stable in the East End but shortly afterwards that site suffered damage as a bomb exploded nearby leaving the stables partially destroyed. Again Upstart did not panic and remained calm until he was led away, this helped the men as an excitable horse can alarm others in the stable and injure those performing the rescue.

Upstart and his rider, District Inspector Morley from Hackney, were out on patrol through the streets of Bethnall Green when a flying bomb exploded 70 yards away. Upstart remained unmoved and did not flinch when the force of the blast sent glass and brick flying through the air around him. Immediately Inspector Morley instructed Upstart to trot toward the bomb site and he responded. The pair were first on the scene and began controlling the traffic and people who gathered in the street. This was important as it allowed the rescue squads and ambulance a quick and easy passage to help the casualties. Without the contribution of Inspector Morley and Upstart more lives could have been lost.

For his calmness when under fire and helping in the rescue of victims of the London Blitz Upstart was awarded the Dickin Medal on 11 April 1947.

Rip

London, 1940

The East End of London was a popular target for Herman Goering's Luftwaffe during the Blitz of London in the early part of the war. A key target was the docks, where so many ships sailed in and out, supplying the nation with food, medicine and weapons. It was here, in September 1940, that an ARP warden, Mr King, found a very scared and hungry dog cowering in an air-raid shelter. Mr King gave the dog some food during the air-raid and then set about finding his owner but sadly no-one came forward. It appeared that the dog had been abandoned or his owner killed.

Mr King felt that the fully-grown animal might leave after he was given more food and some water, but Rip appeared keen to remain with his new master and rewarded his kindness by staying by his side as he completed his work around the docks. Mr King described how valuable his new companion was:

He was very valuable in helping us to locate persons trapped in the debris. During the alerts, heavy gunfire and incendiary raids Rip was always out on duty – never in the way – but always eager to do his bit.

Rip became the most important asset to the Civil Defence Unit as he was the first dog to alert the wardens to buried casualties in a bomb site. Prior to Rip, the wardens would try to listen for cries or tapping from buried survivors but, joining Mr King so early in the war, Rip became the most effective warning system for finding buried people. The War Office was alerted to this talent and set up a specific training school for dogs who were then adopted as working mascots across all types of Civil Defence units. The kindness of Mr King to a cowering dog was rewarded with the saving of many lives, not just by Rip but also by those dogs that followed his lead.

Plate 6 shows Rip in action alerting a warden to a buried boy in what was his home, the victim of another vicious air raid on the East End. Mr King describes Rip's training:

Official dogs are now trained for this kind of work, but Rip was the first dog to locate trapped persons. He had over five years' active service to his credit. Rip's training was done the hard way. When I came across Rip sniffing around on the job, I always knew that there was someone trapped in the ruins.

Rip's age was unknown and he served throughout the war saving many lives, but in the autumn of 1946 he fell ill and died, having developed dropsy, an illness where a high level of fluid develops in body cavities or tissues. Rip was awarded the Dickin Medal for saving the lives of many East End people and without his help Britain may not have deployed more dogs to the ARP units to save others. Rip's contribution, being the first dog to perform such a rescue, cannot be underestimated.

Regal
London, 1941–44

Regal, a bay gelding, was a police horse who lived up to his name not once but twice as he was awarded his Dickin Medal for *failing* to react. This makes Regal unusual as most of his contemporaries were honoured for their heroic actions, often under difficult circumstances.

Regal was stationed at Muswell Hill stables and during an air raid on the night of 19 April 1941, a cluster of explosive incendiary bombs struck the forage room. The fire spread to the stables but no stable hands or policemen were on duty. Regal was found with flames just feet away from him, but he displayed no sign of panic or distress and was calmly led away to safety. Regal's response was remarkable given the noise, smoke and heat from the fire. If Regal had become distressed he may have endangered the lives of his rescuers and caused the other horses to panic.

Three years later, on 20 July 1944, a flying bomb exploded 20 yards from the stables in Muswell Hill where Regal was housed. This time the bomb damage was considerable and the roof of the stable collapsed onto Regal, who fortunately suffered only minor injuries. Again, Regal was unperturbed and remained in the wreckage of the stable until he was led to safety. The PDSA usually awarded medals to those animals who had displayed courage that went beyond the tasks they were trained for. Regal's citation reads:

Regal was twice in burning stables caused by explosive incendiaries at Muswell Hill. Although receiving minor injuries, being covered by debris and close to the flames, this horse showed no signs of panic.

Regal became a popular animal after the war and was well-known and loved by school children in London. Regal, along with the other Muswell Hill police horses, Renard and Nymph, was transferred from Muswell Hill to Tottenham in 1947. Regal was taken on regular patrols through the streets by his rider Police Constable Hector Poole and the local children used to give up their sweets to feed him, a considerable honour considering that rationing was still in force.

Beauty

London, 1940–45

For being the pioneer dog in locating buried air-raid victims, while serving with a PDSA Rescue Squad.

Beauty or Tipperary Beauty was a wire haired terrier that detected buried victims of the London Blitz. Her owner was Mr Bill Barnett, a superintendent of the People's Dispensary for Sick Animals. Beauty was blessed with an unflappable calm in the arena of noise, from falling buildings and the odour of death, which the Blitz delivered on London night after night.

Yet through these horrors Beauty not only maintained her composure in the face of danger but also continued to fulfil her duties with outstanding courage. Beauty was deployed to scale bombsites during and after the bombing raids and detect any buried people who were still alive. Beauty was unique in two ways. Firstly, she specialised in detecting buried animals rather than adults or children and this talent did not simply stretch to other dogs, Beauty could detect all varieties of pets. Secondly, she had had no training for this type of work. It was a natural talent that saved many animals from a painful and lonely death, one that is particularly remarkable when taking into account she was asked to work in all the noise and chaos that followed a bombing raid. At the start of the war the PDSA funded mobile units for the care of animals injured by bombs or shrapnel. The units were manned by volunteers and called upon dogs to help detect animals after human casualties were identified and cared for. The main duties included scaling over bombsites and damaged buildings to locate and care for injured and homeless animals.

One of Beauty's first successes was to rescue a cat that was buried under a bombed-out building. Mr Barnett was the leader of the rescue squad and began 'working the site'; Beauty accompanied him. During a night of heavy bombing when the squad was digging out debris, Beauty began her own search by digging furiously some distance from the remainder of the crew. Eventually this attracted Mr Barnett and his colleagues and they helped to move away soil and brick until the crew discovered a cat hidden under a submerged table. The cat was rescued and became the first of sixty-three animals to be saved from death by Beauty.

The work was hazardous in many aspects and Beauty was so highly regarded that she was presented with leather boots, a rationed item in those days, to protect her paws and legs, which had become scarred and swollen from clambering over bombsites. In recognition of her heroism she was awarded a Pioneer Medal (usually reserved for humans) and a silver mounted medal (with collar) inscribed 'For Services Rendered' from the Deputy Mayor of Hendon. Beauty was also awarded the freedom of Holland Park in Manchester and all the trees therein (a particularly prestigious award as she was the only dog permitted to run loose in it!). Beauty became well-known in London for her exploits and moonlighted at War Savings parades to raise money for the war effort, often leading them. Then, on 12 January 1945, Beauty was awarded the Dickin Medal. The significance of Beauty's achievements is further enhanced by the impact her work had on the owners of the animals she saved. The people whose houses or workplaces, had been destroyed or damaged by the Blitz were often moved to tears by the survival of their beloved pets and the affect on morale cannot be underestimated.

Sheila

Cheviot Hills, 1941

Sheila was a collie dog; the first winner of the Dickin Medal to be a 'civilian' animal with no connection to a military unit. Sheila was a working sheepdog in Northumberland and avoided the call for animals made by the War Office as she was in a reserved occupation. John Dagg, Shelia's master, was a shepherd and Sheila was doing important work rounding up sheep across the remote Cheviot Hills.

On 7 December 1941 America joined the war after the Japanese bombed Pearl Harbour. As a result many American Air Force units were stationed in Britain and practised flying across the mountains around Northumberland. In December 1941 during a blinding snow storm a USAAF B-17 Flying Fortress Bomber from the 8th Army crashed in the remote Brayden Crags in the Cheviot Hills. Despite the appalling weather a search party was put together of local men who knew the hills well. John Dagg and Sheila volunteered. The party knew if any men had survived the crash, they would not survive the night in the below freezing conditions. As the party reached the top of a hill the visibility was minimal. However, Sheila became excited, as though something unusual was ahead and disappeared into the night.

Sheila found the American airmen sheltering in a small ravine. Realising that Sheila was not alone, the men began to shout for help, but the search party could not hear their cries due to the strong winds. Hearing the call of her master Sheila left the airmen and returned to him. She then led the search party to the ravine where the survivors were sheltering. Without Sheila's presence the search party would not have found the airmen and they would have died from their injuries or hypothermia.

John Dagg was awarded the British Empire Medal for meritorious civilian service worthy of recognition by the Crown. On hearing of Sheila's exploits, the Home Office recommended her for honorary membership of the Allied Forces Mascot Club and the award of a Dickin Medal. In July 1944 a presentation party representing the 8th Air Force and the British Air Council travelled to Northumberland to award the honours. Sheila was not used to the formality of such an event and rolled on her back whilst the medal was pinned to her collar.

Sheila's story is well-known in America as the parents of one of the airmen who died in the crash took great interest in the collie sheepdog that saved the survivors. They wrote to the War Department in Washington and enquired whether they might have one of Sheila's puppies. The request was passed onto the Home Office and then the Allied Forces Mascot Club. When he heard, John Dagg was happy to oblige and a beautiful white collie named Tibby travelled from Northumberland to London from where she was flown to South Carolina and presented to the parents who had lost their son on the night that Sheila saved his comrades.

Peter

London, 1945

Peter was a most unlikely winner of the Animal Victoria Cross. Born in 1941 the collie pup was a handful with a poor reputation, who took great pleasure in fighting with other dogs, destroying anything he could get his paws on and behaved like a 'four-legged gangster'. When, in 1944, the War Office made the appeal for animals, his owner, Mrs Stables, offered Peter to the Ministry of Aircraft Production believing the discipline of service would do him some good.

Called up in September 1944, Peter travelled by train on a third class War Department Railway Warrant to the Ministry's Guard Dog School at Staverton Court in Gloucestershire. Mr Archie Knight was given the responsibility of training this unruly animal to become a guard dog and Peter displayed an ability to learn quickly and sense danger. After completing his training Peter was commended for his calmness under battle conditions and excelling when saving lives in bombing raids. Given the code 'Rescue Dog No. 2664/9288' Peter's work began with Archie Knight in the Civil Defence in Chelsea with a team of fourteen other rescue dogs.

In 1944/5 the main threat from the enemy was Doodlebug rockets, which created huge craters and could damage large areas of housing. The London Region Civil Defence Headquarters organised the rescue dogs so civilians trapped under debris and housing could be pulled out alive. In this work Peter excelled. On one occasion he worked on a bombed site for nine hours without rest and did not refuse anything asked of him by his handler. When Peter was relieved by dogs from other groups, he would have six hours rest before returning to the site where he worked for another two hours. It was said officially of him, 'There is no doubt that the prompt and accurate information he gave to his handler resulted in the saving of human lives.'

On another mission, Peter gave a strong indication to dig in a specific area and the men of the team began removing debris. After a short while a voice could be heard under the soil and brick cursing in colourful language; the digging continued at a furious pace to save the victim below. The last of the wreckage was removed and a large, irate parrot was unearthed clearly annoyed but otherwise in good health.

Amongst Peter's finest work was the detection of two people in early April 1945. Archie Knight kept a diary of his wartime exploits and describes events:

I think one of his finest jobs was on Monday. We were called twenty hours after the incident, and after several hours of heavy rain. Three bodies were missing and he very quickly indicated in a most unlikely spot, but he was right, and they uncovered a man and a woman both on the same spot. After all that rain had packed debris tightly, I thought this a most praiseworthy effort. The next day we were called to another job. There were so many calls for Peter, who is well known in this district that I worked him ten hours and he never once refused to give all he had. All his marks revealed casualties. The next day we returned, and he worked like a hero again, until after six hours, I refused to ask any more of him. I hated to work him like this but I also hated to refuse the rescue parties who were asking for him, he was really played out but he worked like a Trojan.

This passage reveals the effort these animals gave to the war effort and the high regard in which they were held by their handlers. In May 1945 Peter attended the scene of one of the final Doodlebug attacks of the war and saved the life of a young boy who had been buried in the rubble of his house. Peter managed to scour the site and indicate where digging should begin, within minutes the boy was brought to the surface.

Only on one occasion did Peter refuse to work. At the very end of the war he attended a bombsite with a fellow Chelsea Civil Defence dog named Taylor and both animals refused to respond to their handlers' numerous promptings. After a period of time they were both withdrawn and, thinking they must be unwell, were sent back to headquarters. Taylor's handler, Mr Rowe, and Archie could not fathom this isolated act of defiance until Rowe realised that due to enemy action the meat ration for the dogs had not been delivered and they had been fed biscuits for three days. With no meat the dogs thought they were on a holiday.

After the war had ended Peter was retained by the Civil Defence Unit to lead a parade in Hyde Park in the presence of the king and queen, and Princess Elizabeth. Peter was far from overawed by this honour and took great interest in the queen's fur coat rather than the ceremony or the prestigious company, the king remarked, 'He must think it's a rabbit, my dear.'

Peter spent the post-war years as a mountain rescue dog and giving demonstrations at Staverton Court. On 12 November 1945 he was chosen as a recipient of the Dickin Medal for saving the lives of six people buried in the rubble of London. A tremendous achievement for the unruly pup Mrs Stables gave up in 1944.

Peter died in November 1952 at the People's Dispensary for Sick Animals in Nottingham and was buried in the Animal Cemetery in Ilford Essex with a Union Jack draped around his coffin.

Olga
Tooting, 1944

On duty when a flying bomb demolished four houses in Tooting and a plate-glass window crashed immediately in front of her. Olga, after bolting for 100 yards, returned to the scene of the incident and remained on duty with her rider, controlling traffic and assisting rescue organisations.

Olga was a twelve-year-old bay mare who served with the Metropolitan Police during the war and was the last horse to win the Dickin Medal. On 1 July 1944 Olga was patrolling Tooting with her temporary rider for the day, Police Constable J.E. Thwaites, as her usual handler was on other duties. A Doodlebug was passing overhead when the engine cut out. The people of London knew from experience that this would send the flying bomb hurtling uncontrollably to the ground. This weapon was capable of killing a large number of people, inflicting terrible injuries and causing huge material damage to buildings and homes. The missile exploded on impact with the ground, and a huge blast wave rippled out from the epicentre. As it did so it left a vacuum, which caused a second rush of air as the vacuum was filled triggering a devastating pushing and pulling effect. On the fringes of the blast-zone windows and doors would be ripped out and shrapnel would be propelled through the air.

Olga and Police Constable Thwaites were close enough to the crash site to feel the force of the blast as four houses were demolished. Glass and debris covered a 75-yard area. Olga, who was startled, as a plate glass window smashed at her feet, bolted 100 yards, still with PC Thwaites on her back. PC Thwaites calmed Olga and managed to persuade her to return to the site, making him the first officer on the scene. Olga then displayed exemplary behaviour and assisted with the search and rescue attempt, controlling traffic and excluding people who gathered around the crash site.

Olga was awarded the Dickin Medal on 11 April 1947 for her return to the scene and the crucial work in the immediate aftermath of the explosion.

Irma

London, 1944–45

Upon the outbreak of war the government and War Office was sceptical about the use of dogs to seek out people and bodies from the wreckage of a bombed-out building. It was felt that after a bomb had been dropped and damaged a building the combination of smells would confuse the animal. Bombing raids smashed buildings leaving dust, soot and the burning smell of wood, paint and metal. Gas and sewage pipes were also destroyed, creating a mix of odours that would confuse an animal seeking to sniff out a corpse or a trapped civilian under the ground. This book has already examined the role Beauty played in changing that view and Irma, along with the contribution of Mrs Margaret Griffin, also made a significant contribution.

The Air Ministry was impressed with the work of Beauty and other dogs trained to guard airfields and military installations and decided to create a small guard dog school under the command of Colonel Baldwin. There was very little money for the venture and the volunteers, Margaret Griffin, Charles Fricker and Bill Barrow, helped build kennels and set up a training programme. Margaret would take her puppy along with her whilst she helped set up the school. The puppy's name was Irma. Margaret was a well-known breeder and Irma's family tree was impressive; her father was Storm and grandmother was Echo who had already distinguished themselves. It was not long before Irma was enlisted at the training school and she excelled, with a special gift for being able to detect whether the casualty was alive or dead. This skill was something the other dogs could not manage and Irma developed a system to alert her handlers. If the casualty was still alive Irma would bark, if dead she would sit down and wag her tail.

Irma and Margaret were deployed in London to seek casualties from the Doodlebug raids. Margaret kept a detailed record of their efforts and that of another rescue dog named Psyche, which illustrates the effort and bravery of the team.

30.10.1944 – Call at 01:20 hrs (1.20 am) to Maryland Point, West Ham. Irma put in at once. She took me through to a cellar where three kiddies were trapped. Rescue got to work on this place at once, but the children died before they could be reached through the heavy debris.

21.11.1944 – Rocket on Walthamstowe, 12:30 hrs. Arrived on site 13:30 hrs. Four houses completely demolished, about twelve badly knocked about. Things were made no easier by water pipes burst in all directions and a bad gas leak under the debris. A smashed meter was pouring gas into the rubble. Worked Irma. In spite of the stench of gas, she indicated at a point at the back of the debris. From the front of building, she and I went right under the floors crawling on our stomachs in water. She lay down here when we reached a point approximately dead below the spot where she had indicated. Below this the bodies of a woman and two children were buried 4ft under fine rubble and dust.

It is often the animals who gain credit for their work detecting buried casualties but the bravery shown by Margaret entering such a dangerous site and risking her life to save others must also be recognised as most courageous.

20.1.1945 – Call to Osbourne Road, Tottenham at 21:00 hrs. In house No. 1 Irma found two live casualties. In No. 2 Irma again gave good indication just to one side of a fairly large and fierce fire burning through collapsed house debris. Thick smoke rising here. Family of five found. In No. 3 a strong indication from Irma over the debris. Rescue found a live cat.

27.1.1945 – Bitterly cold. Snowing [Back to the Gordon Road incident at West Ham]. I went in under the floor cavity (of Nos 90–92) with the dogs. Psyche whined and went down. Irma scratched below me in rubble and found bed clothing here. Advised digging this out first. Rescue party put onto this and excavation gave bodies of one adult female and one adult male. From here I was asked to try over at No. 94 and Irma examined round about and told me there was someone there. Taking the wind into account I advised working a bit back from indication point up into wind. Rescue did so. At 4 feet back was found the body of one adult female.

On another occasion Irma had given a 'live' signal by barking loudly when crossing some debris and began scratching at the ground. The rescue team set to work immediately such was their faith in Irma.

After digging and removing wreckage the team were distraught to find a lifeless body, however after resuscitation the casualty recovered consciousness. Often many dead were carried past Irma as they were excavated from the earth and she would lick their faces or hands and look up at her handler as if something should be done about it.

In March 1945 Margaret was called to a site on the morning following a bombing raid as there were still people unaccounted for. Irma and Psyche together suddenly ran to a point in the debris. Beneath this rubble the team found a collapsed floor under which a woman was trapped. She had been there nine hours and was still conscious, but had cradled her dead son in the darkness. Irma and Psyche had detected the scent of the woman in a concealed location as rescue workers had been walking over the area and the position of the floors was quite unsuspected. A few feet away Irma then located another victim. Upon removing the rubble a small cavity was exposed and out jumped a small collie dog vigorously shaking her coat to remove the dust. More often than not the rescue teams were faced with removing corpses from what were people's homes; the sight of unearthing a living animal unharmed must have been a tremendous feeling.

In total the Irma-Psyche rescue team located 233 people during the latter years of the war. Of those, Irma found twenty-one alive and 170 dead on her own, a record number for which Irma was awarded the Dickin Medal. Margaret Griffin was awarded the British Empire Medal for her bravery and courage escorting Irma endlessly in dangerous circumstances.

Jet
London, 1944–45

Jet is one of a small number of animals to win the highest award for animal bravery from both the PDSA and the RSPCA. Sometimes known as Jet of Iada after his mother, the bitch Iada Dilah of Lilias, who had a large litter of which Jet was one puppy. A pure black Alsatian who had a natural talent for detecting those buried under ground, both dead and alive, he was one of the first dogs to be trained at the RAF School for Police Dogs in Gloucester. Born and bred in Liverpool by the renowned dog breeder Mrs Babcock Cleaver, Jet's ability was quickly noticed by Mrs Griffin who became a brilliant trainer of war dogs.

The first examples of Jet's talents were witnessed during an air-raid in Birmingham shortly after he left the training school. A rubber factory targeted by enemy aircraft suffered a direct hit, leaving the building a smouldering ruin. Jet was asked to scour the area for casualties and quickly indicated a spot. The men of the rescue party began removing machinery, bricks and soil but could not find any human remains, however Jet returned and selected the same location. Reluctantly the party started to dig again, with each spade full of brick and soil they became less convinced a casualty rested below until they came across a badly burned body 25 feet below the surface. This remarkable discovery attracted attention and Jet was selected, along with another dog named Irma, to work in London for the Civil Defence Unit who responded to attacks from Doodlebugs. If the casualty was alive, Jet would quickly become agitated and try to get to the person.

In September 1944 Jet was called into action in London alongside his handler Corporal Wardle from the RAF. Never keen to leave home, Jet was also a poor traveller and he was unwell for most of the car journey but upon arriving he had less than two hours rest when a call came from Edmonton. A bomb had destroyed a house and the owner was trapped under the debris. Jet arrived and scoured the site before sitting down and whining. The dead body was unearthed shortly afterwards.

In Chelsea during October 1944 came the incident that led to Jet's recommendation for the Dickin Medal. A large hotel was partially destroyed. The Civil Defence teams had spent hours helping survivors to safety and were about to stand down but Jet, who had been working constantly for eleven-and-a-half hours, refused to budge. A search was instigated but no-one else was found, Jet continued to indicate that someone was alive in the ruined hotel and attempted to scale the rubble. Ladders were brought and high up in the upper floors, on a ledge, rested a sixty-three-year-old woman covered in white plaster. She was rescued, taken to hospital and made a swift recovery.

On another occasion Jet was called to the site of a hospital that had been partially destroyed by a bomb and set about scrambling over the debris in search of patients and staff. After twelve hours non-stop work Jet was still sniffing and scratching on the ground, suddenly he stopped, pointed his nose upwards and would not remove his gaze from the roof. The men of the rescue team were puzzled then realised he was glaring at part of the roof that was still standing. The fire brigade arrived and up they went to the roof where they found an elderly patient who had been thrown into the rafters by the explosion. Along with his partner Irma, they discovered over fifty casualties in under six weeks during the worst of the Doodlebug bombings.

After the war had ended Jet was in demand again in 1947. Mrs Cleaver received a telephone call requesting Jet to go down the Whitehaven mine to retrieve the bodies of those killed in the mining disaster. Some 117 victims perished after an explosion ripped apart a mine in Whitehaven but many were missing and the relatives requested the help of Jet (as well as two other dogs, Prince and Rex) to retrieve their loved ones. The grief-stricken town had begun an inquest into the sixty-four bodies already recovered and relatives were summoned to identify their loved ones. The stretch of mine that Jet was requested to search was a 2,000-yard-long tunnel deep underground that was unstable after the collapse.

As Jet guided the rescue party along the tunnel he suddenly stopped in his tracks and whined. Jet then moved a few paces back and sat down on the tunnel floor and looked up, the men stared at him bewildered. Jet's handler asked everyone to move back. Almost immediately the section of tunnel that Jet continued to glare at collapsed in front of them. Once the rock had been cleared Jet led the rescue party toward the remaining miners' bodies and a rescue was completed.

The government made a careful record of all the successes and failures of each dog used during the war and selected Jet and Irma as those who were most successful. For rescuing civilians from under the rubble of their own homes during the final months of the war, Jet received the Dickin Medal, which was awarded on 12 January 1945. For warning the rescue party of the imminent collapse of a mine shaft in Whitehaven he was awarded the Star of Whitehaven and the RSPCA Medal of Honour. Jet passed away in October 1949 and is buried beneath a sundial memorial in the Rose Garden in Liverpool's Calderstone Park. In 1971 the comedian Ken Dodd unveiled a luxurious memorial kennel in Jet's honour at the RSPCA Animal Home in Liverpool.

Thorn

London, 1944–45

Thorn was an Alsatian with a family history to rival most, an instructor in mine detection, a Dickin Medal winner and then a film star. Thorn was the great-grandson of Echo, bred by Mrs Griffin, and was also related to the other Alsatian Dickin Medal winner, Irma. Mrs Griffin was a well-known breeder of pedigree dogs renowned for their character and fortitude. Echo completed a year of service as a patrol dog during the war and was absent for just one night due to a laceration above the eye.

Thorn began military life by going through training with the Ministry of Aircraft Production School, handled by Mr Russell. After training, at which Thorn excelled, he became an instructor demonstrating to other dogs how to detect mines, complete a mountain rescue and how to lead people from buildings for the Air Raid Precaution Service. Thorn was enlisted to accompany the PDSA Rescue squads whose motto was 'The PDSA goes where the bombs fall'. Thorn would be allowed to explore the bombsites, burning buildings and wreckage first to detect buried people. On one occasion, in tandem with Jet, they found no fewer than twenty-five people buried in South London. The dogs would scour the bombsites, begin sniffing and then scratch away at the surface to unearth the buried person.

Thorn was called to the site where a V-bomb had exploded and left, in its wake, the burning shell of a building. Procedure dictated that one dog and handler would be allowed into the building to appraise the situation and to attempt detection of life. Thorn entered slowly and Mr Russell described events:

We were working on houses that were on fire. One dog refused to go into the smoke. Thorn went in slowly, step-by-step. He repeatedly flinched, but encouraged on, he reached a spot approximately over the seat of the fire. There he gave positive indication of having found someone and casualties were recovered from this spot. In my opinion the work of Thorn on this occasion was the best I have seen from any rescue dog. I personally found it impossible to see in the smoke and had to be helped down to where the air was clearer.

Mr Russell was awarded the British Empire Medal for his bravery and Thorn received the Dickin Medal. Without the bravery of Thorn the people in the building would have died from asphyxiation. Let us not forget that one patrol dog had refused to go in and had Thorn not been present human lives would have been lost. Despite the heat from the fire, noise of sirens and further explosions during the bombing, Thorn entered a building despite being scared. In total he rescued over 100 human casualties during his service. On 25 April 1945 Thorn and Mr Russell travelled to Wembley Stadium to receive their medals.

Usually at this point in the lives of medal winners they return to their pre-war families and slip into retirement to live out their lives as pets. However, Thorn went on to have a career as a film star. Thorn's relative, Echo, starred in the film *Master and Man* and Thorn him-self had a role alongside Anne Crawford and Maxwell Reed in *Unholy Innocent* based on the play *They Walk Alone*. In the film Miss Crawford and Thorn tracked down a murderer who had killed his master; needless to say, they caught the villain redhanded. After this film Thorn was insured for £1,000 and commanded a sum of £75 per film appearance for roles in *And So To Work* and *The Captive Heart*. Thorn was even given a stuffed 'stunt' double, which he did not take kindly to.

During the war Thorn survived bombs, fires and collapsing buildings but one day in Hever he went for a walk with Mr Russell across farmland. Thorn saw some sheep and dashed after them, unknown to Mr Russell the farmer had lost four sheep to an un-known dog and believed Thorn was the offender and fired his shotgun. Thorn was hit and fell to the ground. Mr Russell rushed to him, Thorn had been hit by a bullet in the shoulder and there was a lot of blood. Mr Russell rushed him to medical help, an operation was quickly organised to remove the bullet, but he was not expected to survive. For five days Mr Russell remained with Thorn. After a week Thorn began to make a recovery and lived out his retirement.

PART 3

MODERN HEROES

Sam

The former Yugoslavia, 1998

For outstanding gallantry during conflict in Bosnia-Herzegovina while assigned to the Royal Canadian Regiment in Drvar, his true valour undoubtedly saved the lives of many servicemen and civilians.

The state of Yugoslavia, created after the First World War, became a mix of ethnic races, religions and languages and was dissolved in 1991. Soon after the tensions between these races erupted into violence and war ensued. The United Nations occupied the region as a peacekeeping force whilst Serb and Croats continued disputes against a backdrop of ethnic cleansing. It was against this backdrop that Sam won his Dickin Medal.

Sam, a German Shepherd, was a member of the Royal Canadian Regiment with handler Sergeant Iain Carnegie stationed in the town of Drvar as part of a peacekeeping force. Trained as a patrol and guard dog, Sam displayed two acts of initiative and extreme bravery beyond expectations for an army dog. The first came on 18 April 1998 when Sam and his handler were called into action after reports of a man firing a gun in the town of Drvar. Upon arriving in the town they were called into a bar where the man was shooting a pistol. Sam went first and located the man, wrestling him to the ground whilst Sergeant Carnegie disarmed him. The actions of Sam prevented further shootings and no-one was hurt.

On 24 April, Sam and Corporal Carnegie were called to a warehouse compound. A Bosnian Muslim mob had surrounded a warehouse in which over fifty Serb civilians had taken refuge. The atmosphere was extremely volatile and the mob attempted to gain entry to the warehouse through windows and the main entrance in order to attack the people inside. Sergeant Carnegie and Sam arrived and immediately took up a position at the main entrance acting as a barricade. The mob reacted furiously with a hail of rocks and missiles as they laid siege to the building. Despite suffering numerous injuries from these attacks, Sam and Sergeant Carnegie held firm and were relieved by reinforcements. The Serb civilians inside were unharmed due to their courage and bravery.

Sam passed away, aged ten, from natural causes shortly after leaving the army. Sergeant Carnegie received Sam's posthumous Dickin Medal and stated, 'Sam displayed outstanding courage and not once did he shy away from danger. I could never have carried out my duties without Sam at my side. He deserves the best.' Sam was the first army dog to win the award since 1944 and was the 59th recipient.

Salty, Roselle and Apollo
New York, 9/11

On 11 September 2001, the World Trade Center in New York came under attack from terrorists who had seized control of passenger flights and flew them directly into each tower, resulting in the total destruction of each building and the loss of thousands of lives. Salty and Roselle won Dickin Medals on this day. They were not rescue animals but guide dogs for the blind.

Michael Hingson worked on the 78th floor in Tower One as a sales manager for Quantum, and was accompanied to work each day by Roselle who sat under his desk. When the first plane struck the building, chaos ensued with people charging toward the lifts and staircases. The deafening noise, the smoke and heat from the explosions added to the confusion. Roselle did not panic but calmly rose from under the desk to lead Michael to the nearest staircase. Despite the heat and difficulty breathing, they descended the stairs together with Roselle guiding Michael past wreckage and fire all the way to the bottom. Other workers followed the pair and many lives were saved as the smoke made visibility impossible.

Once outside, Roselle guided Michael into nearby streets. She then walked with her owner through the cloud of smoke and debris after Tower One collapsed, and even helped to lead others who were blinded and confused in the choking dust and ash. Without Roselle, Michael Hingson would have died in the attack and many others would not have made their way down the stairs to safety.

Omar Rivera worked on the 71st floor in Tower One for the Port Authority and his guide dog, Salty, also used to rest under his desk whilst he worked. When the first plane struck the building Omar was aware of what had happened as fellow workers were shouting. Feeling that he had no chance of escape, he decided to unleash Salty so at least the animal could have an opportunity to survive. Salty left the side of his owner but within moments he returned of his own volition to guide his owner to the stairs.

Salty began to lead Omar down the stairs but also managed to help a female worker, Miss Donna Enright who was struggling down the stairs; she had also been on the 78th floor and had been blinded by flying debris when the plane exploded. For the next one hour and fifteen minutes, Salty carefully guided the pair down seventy-one crowded flights of stairs. Despite the overpowering stench of jet fuel, the splinters of glass and debris underfoot and ankle-deep water, Salty never hesitated or faltered.

Salty and Roselle were awarded the Animal Victoria Cross for their bravery in saving the lives of many victims of the 9/11 attacks on the World Trade Center. Each dog displayed courage beyond their training as guide dogs for the blind.

On 5 March 2002 Apollo, a German Shepherd, and handler Pete Davis, a police officer, accepted the Dickin Medal on behalf of all Search and Rescue dogs who worked at Ground Zero and at the Pentagon. The citation on the medal reads:

For tireless courage in the service of humanity during the search and rescue operations in New York and Washington on and after 11 September 2001. Faithful to words of command and undaunted by the task, the dogs' work and unstinting devotion to duty stand as a testament to those lost or injured.

Treo

Afghanistan, 2008

Treo, from the 104th Military Working Dog Support Unit, is the most recent winner of the Dickin Medal. As a puppy Treo was close to being put down as he was badly behaved; biting and barking at anyone who came near him. However, he was enlisted as an army dog and intensive army training saved him, but his handler left the army. Treo then met his new handler and they immediately became inseparable. From this moment on, Treo became a 'four legged metal detector' and, with Sergeant Dave Heyhoe, was first sent to Northern Ireland then to Afghanistan.

The war in Afghanistan, particularly in Helmand Province, involved skirmishes between the Taliban and the British Army. To counter the progress made by British troops, the Taliban began to experiment with different weapons that would inflict maximum damage whilst avoiding actual engagement with their enemy. Posted in March 2008, Treo was deployed in Helmand Province after training as a sniffer dog; his role was to detect mines buried beneath the desert and roadside bombs. With his handler, Treo would save many lives.

On 15 August 2008, Heyhoe and Treo were on patrol down a pathway in Sangin, in fifty degree heat alongside a riverbank near a British Army compound. Treo suddenly started to behave in a different manner than usual; he put his nose in the air then back down to the sandy surface before sucking like a vacuum. Heyhoe realised he was onto something and over the next few minutes Treo detected a daisy chain of Improvised Explosive Devices (IEDs) all along the path. A daisy chain bomb is one that requires just one device to be activated and all those connected will explode in sequence. There was enough explosive to destroy the camp and kill up to forty servicemen and women. Treo's discovery was the first time the British Army had faced IED daisy chains so close to a military base and alerted troops to a new threat, thus saving many more lives in the future. In September 2008, Treo found a second daisy chain which, if left unearthed, would have been guaranteed to lead to casualties from 7 Platoon, the Royal Irish Regiment.

During his tour of duty Treo was equipped with his own pack to help combat the searing heat and dusty conditions; his body armour contained ice packs to keep him cool and he had four shoes to protect his paws as he moved through rough terrain. Heyhoe even built Treo a special kennel but he always refused to sleep in it, preferring his handler's bed.

Treo received his medal from Princess Alexandra on 24 February 2010 at the Imperial War Museum in London. Treo is still alive today, living out a peaceful retirement in Lincolnshire where he spends his time chewing top quality bones from a local butcher and watching Manchester City on the television, whilst sitting in his very own reclining chair.

Sadie
Afghanistan, 2005

The United Nations set up a headquarters in Kabul, the capital of Afghanistan, from which they governed the Allied occupied regions of the country. Any military base or administration centre was vulnerable to attack from the Taliban and their choice of weapon was often devastating, particularly as they had developed a technique of leaving a second bomb at the same site as the first. This was designed to act as insurance should the first bomb be discovered and to ensure more devastation when military personnel arrive to help rescue those injured from the first device.

It is into this battleground that Lance Corporal Karen Yardley and Sadie, a black Labrador, were thrust. Attached to the Royal Gloucestershire, Berkshire and Wiltshire Light Infantry Regiment, Lance Corporal Yardley and Sadie were on patrol around the streets of Kabul on 14 November 2005. They were called to the United Nations headquarters to help survivors of a suicide blast outside the building. Aware of the threat of a second explosion Corporal Yardley and Sadie set to work. At this stage it was unknown whether a second suicide bomber would appear or whether an explosive was buried beneath the streets.

Sadie detected the scent of an explosive device and intimated with such speed that it was inside the wall of the headquarters building that a safe evacuation was completed. To detect the smell through a thick concrete wall was remarkable and Corporal Yardley started a search that ended shortly afterwards when the device was discovered hidden in a wall cavity. Corporal Yardley described the search: 'As Sadie went towards the compound's wall onto the street she picked up a scent. She sat down and stared directly at the wall, which meant there was something right on the other side. I immediately shouted for everyone to get out of the area.'

The explosive device was timed to detonate and cause maximum loss of life of those working inside the building and those outside on the busy street. Sadie's quick detection gave bomb disposal experts the time required to defuse the device and prevent the death or injury of hundreds of civilians as well as British, American and German soldiers who were tending to the wounded civilians.

Sadie was the 25th dog to be awarded the Dickin Medal when HRH Princess Alexandra presented the medal on 6 February 2006 at the Imperial War Museum in London.

The citation on her medal read:

Sadie gave a positive indication near a concrete blast wall and multi-national personnel were moved to a safe distance. At the site of Sadie's indication, bomb disposal operators later made safe an explosive device. The bomb was designed to inflict maximum injury.

Buster

Iraq, 2003

Buster was a brown and white springer spaniel assigned to the Royal Army Veterinary Corps whilst serving in Iraq during 2003. Buster was an unwanted pup and rescued from the Battersea Dogs Home by the Morgan family. Sergeant Danny Morgan, his master, also became his handler and served with him in Iraq.

In April 2003 a dawn raid on the village of Safwan, in the southern region of Iraq was scheduled. In such circumstances sniffer dogs move ahead of troops to search for roadside bombs or hidden explosives; Buster was moving through the streets of Safwan ahead of Sergeant Morgan. The village was suspected of housing insurgents and terrorists who were said to have a hold over the local community. After a short time Buster became very excited and the men of the patrol moved in and located a group of insurgents in a house. The insurgents denied having any weapons or explosives.

A manual search of the building took place but no arms were found. At this point Buster again became very excited in front of a wardrobe. Sergeant Morgan understood this was the signal Buster gave when he thought he had found weapons or explosives and describes events:

Buster found their arms even though they were hidden in a wall cavity, covered with a sheet of tin then with a wardrobe pushed in front of it ... We'd never have found the weapons without him and they would still be a threat to the troops and the local population.

The wall cavity contained explosives, bomb making equipment, propaganda, arms, drugs, grenades and ammunition. The insurgents were arrested and the peaceful confiscation of this arsenal undoubtedly saved lives. The local population of Safwan became much more relaxed after the raid was completed, and troops were able to patrol the streets of the village without heavy armour for the first time.

Buster had succeeded where humans failed and was the 60th recipient of the Dickin Medal.

PART 4

FOREIGN HEROES

G.I. Joe
Italy, 1943

G.I. Joe (U.S.A. 43SC6390) was a dark-chequered pied white pigeon that was hatched in Algiers, Algeria on 24 March 1943 and later enlisted into the United States Army Pigeon Service as one of over 54,000 recruits. Serving first in Tunisia and later Birzerte, G.I. Joe was then taken to the Italian front.

As the battle for the control of Italy raged, a British force, the 56th London Infantry Division, made a big push and succeeded in penetrating the German line, driving the enemy back. The tried and trusted method deployed by the Allies was to use air strikes against the towns and villages that were German strongholds and then attack with troops on the ground. The 56th London Division was scheduled to attack the city of Colvi Vecchia at 10:00 hrs on 18 October 1943. Prior to this the US Air Support Command was scheduled to bomb the city to soften the entrance for the troops.

The British entered the city ahead of schedule after the Germans retreated to reform a defensive line. They left a small rear guard force, which was quickly disabled as the 56th Division gained control of the city. Unfortunately attempts to cancel the scheduled bombing raid failed as radio communication was down and a runner would not be able to reach the airfield many miles away in time. In another twenty minutes the city was due to be bombed. The 56th Division commanders had a decision to make; they could withdraw from the city and hand back control of Colvi Vecchia to the German forces as well as the tactical initiative or release a pigeon in the hope that the bird could cover the 20 miles in twenty minutes with a message to cancel the bombing raid. G.I. Joe was selected and sent off with the message. Once the bombers were airborne the raid could not have been cancelled so G.I. Joe was the only hope. The commanders did not inform the civilians or the men of the 56th Division for fear of spreading panic. They sat tight and waited.

On the runway at the US Air Support Command base the bombers, laden with explosives, were circling into formation order to prepare for take off when G.I. Joe flew over the last mountains and arrowed in toward his loft. The bombers were moving down the runway as the message was removed from his leg, once the men read the message they ran out to the planes to halt take off. G.I. Joe had made it in time. He had covered the 20 miles in twenty minutes.

G.I. Joe saved the lives of the British troops and Italian civilians. General Mark Clark, Commander the US Fifth Army, estimated that the pigeon saved at least 1,000 men of the 56th Division. In the modern world it is difficult to imagine the wellbeing of so many men resting on the exploits of a pigeon when such sophisticated technology is at our finger tips. Let us not forget that the radio equipment was broken and G.I. Joe was set a task no other creature nor human could undertake. Not only that, he completed the feat in under the twenty minutes required and saved a great many lives.

The Dickin Medal was awarded to G.I. Joe in August 1946 and his citation reads:

> *This bird is credited with making the most outstanding flight by a USA army pigeon in the Second World War. It made the 20-mile flight from British 10th Army HQ in the same number of minutes. It brought a message which arrived just in time to save the lives of at least 100 Allied soldiers from being bombed by their own planes.*

After the war G.I. Joe became a national hero in America as he was the first American creature to win the Dickin Medal. He was housed in the Churchill Loft, otherwise known as the Hall of Fame, in New Jersey with twenty-four other heroic pigeons. In March 1957 G.I. Joe was moved to the Detroit Zoological Gardens to see out his retirement. It was here that he passed away at the age of eighteen years on 3 June 1961. G.I. Joe was mounted and is now on display in the Historical Centre at Fort Monmouth, New Jersey, still a hero for those twenty minutes.

Punch and Judy
Jerusalem, 1946

Punch and Judy were brother and sister Boxer dogs owned by Lieutenant Colonel Campbell, the Deputy Judge Advocate General of Jerusalem, and Lieutenant Colonel Niven. In 1946, the two men were living in a suburb of Jerusalem, Palestine. This was a particularly violent period in the history of the Middle East, the product of two decades of Jewish migration into Arab lands.

Violence had erupted during the 1920s and 1930s but Jewish migration continued. It became particularly fervent with Adolf Hitler's rise to power which encouraged Jews to flee Germany. For the Arabs there were two enemies; the Jews and the British authorities based in Palestine via their League of Nations mandate. For the Jews there were also two enemies; the Arabs and the British. The latter hoped to appease the Arabs in the region but also keep on side with the Jews by recognising that Jews could enter Palestine, but in restricted numbers. This policy failed and both Jews and Arabs continued to attack British troops and buildings, the worst of which came with the terrorist bombing of the King David Hotel in Jerusalem on 22 July 1946, where the offices of the British government in Palestine were located. Chaos reigned with the repeated attacks and tensions rose. The British imposed a curfew between nightfall and sunrise with sentries given license to shoot on sight.

On a warm August evening, Campbell and Niven were talking in their living room with Punch and Judy lying peacefully at their feet. The front door was open and a breeze gently moved through the house. At 10.30 pm the two men decided to go to bed and, as was usual, they took a look around the house and garden before retiring; something they did each evening.

Unknown to the men a terrorist lurked in the garden armed with a machine gun aimed at the front door. When the men moved into sight the terrorist planned to open fire on them both. As the two men rose from their chairs and moved along the hall towards the front door, Punch and Judy leaped up and started barking before running out of the house into the garden. Before Campbell and Niven could reach for their weapons and follow the dogs, they heard a burst of machine gun fire and a yelp of pain. As the men reached the garden

65

it was clear the terrorist had fled after spraying the front door with machine gun fire. Punch and Judy were nowhere to be seen. They then noticed a trail of blood leading out onto the street, which they immediately followed. Police and military units arrived quickly and joined Campbell and Niven in the search.

Punch was found lying in a pool of blood, he had been hit four times; twice in the throat, one bullet had left a four inch gash on his skull, the fourth bullet had struck Punch under the right groin. Next to him they found Judy, also covered in blood. The terrorist was nowhere to be seen. Immediately a telephone message was put through to the superintendent of the PDSA in Jerusalem in the hope he would travel, despite the curfew, to treat Punch and Judy. Fortunately, he arrived safely and found Punch laid out on a table to make him as comfortable as possible but he had lost three quarters of a pint of blood and stood very little chance of recovery. Nevertheless, the superintendent set to work giving Punch injections and treating his wounds. To the relief of Campbell and Niven, Punch responded to the treatment.

Judy was then examined, and remarkably was unharmed except for a long graze along her back. The superintendent guessed that she must have lain across Punch to protect him, perhaps from a further attack by the terrorist, and became covered in blood.

Punch and Judy both survived the attack and prevented the death of the two British officers by reacting to the danger before Campbell and Niven, who were unaware that the terrorist was approaching. They received their medals in November 1946 and the citation reads:

These dogs saved the lives of two British Officers in Israel by attacking an armed terrorist who was stealing upon them unawares and thus warning them of their danger. Punch sustained 4 bullet wounds and Judy a long graze down her back.

DD43Q879
Papua New Guinea, 1944

Manus Island is in northern Papua New Guinea and is covered in rugged jungle, which can be broadly described as lowland tropical rain forest. In 1942, Japan established a military base on Manus Island that was attacked by United States forces based in the Admiralty Islands campaign of February/March 1944. They were supported by the British Pacific Fleet based at the Allied naval base at Seeadler Harbour and a small Australian pigeon with no name but a code, DD 43Q879, who would win the Dickin Medal. Fighting a way into the interior where the mountain range would provide defensive positions and through the swampy forests covering the rest of the island would not be easy. Only four roads existed on the island so the attack was made, painstakingly, over jungle terrain.

Bred by the Australian Voluntary Pigeon Service, DD43Q879 was borrowed by the US Marines for the attack on Manus Island. A group of Marines was sent to patrol the village of Dravito and took this pigeon with them. The situation on the island at this time was tense. The strength of the Japanese forces was not known and the Marines feared a counter attack against their advancing troops. Whilst patrolling the area they came across a large contingent of Japanese troops, obviously preparing for a counter attack. The Marines were in a perilous position; the Japanese attacked Dravito with the aim of killing all the men in the patrol to prevent the secret of the counter offensive becoming known.

As a hail of bullets and bombs rained down on the village, the Marines radio was damaged and would not work. The men tried to repair it so that they could call for air support but it was beyond salvaging. Japanese soldiers kept the patrol pinned down and encircled the village. The Marines had only one option and that was to release the two pigeons they were carrying with a message for Allied headquarters. Each bird had a message warning of an impending Japanese attack and a plea for support. As they were released the first pigeon was immediately shot down, the second bird, DD43Q879, managed to evade the bullets as the Japanese intensified their assault on the village.

The Marines were in a desperate position, outnumbered by an aggressive enemy and pinned down. Their only hope in this tight situation was the message carried by the Australian pigeon and time was short as the Japanese were closing in on the patrol. In just thirty minutes DD43Q879 covered the 46 miles from Dravito to the Allied HQ, despite the battle raging on the ground. The Allied forces wasted no time and heavily bombed the surrounding area of Dravito and prepared defences for the Japanese counter attack. The men of the patrol managed to escape under the cover of heavy bombardment.

Without DD43Q879 the men on the patrol would have most probably been killed by the Japanese or captured and tortured. The actions of this bird helped save many lives when the information of a counter attack by enemy forces was relayed back to the Allied headquarters. As a result the pigeon was awarded the Dickin Medal for:

Carrying an SOS message under heavy fire, which brought relief to a patrol of US Marines cut off by Japanese on Manus Island.

Tich

North Africa and Italy, 1940–45

*There were many men who in a tight corner were very materially
helped to keep their heads and their sense of proportion by the
courageous example of one small dog.*

These were the words of Lieutenant Colonel Williams describing
Tich, a black Egyptian mongrel with some Dachshund thrown in
who was born in Cairo and picked up as a stray in Africa by the
1st Battalion of the King's Royal Rifle Corps. As the Corps moved
through the African desert they approached Algiers and came
across many unwanted animals who had been deserted by their
owners. In time of war many animals were left homeless as a result
of bombing raids or due to their owners being killed. Many family
pets were simply turfed out into the street as food was scarce. Tich
was one such animal, and like many others they attached themselves to troops for food.

Tich was seen following the regiment as they moved through the
hills near Algiers and the British troops could not bear to see an
animal so thin and under-nourished so they fed her with scraps of
food. As Rifleman Thomas Walker began to feed Tich scraps of food,
his Arab owner came out of a nearby house and began speaking to
the British troops. A deal was quickly struck to swap Tich for a cup
of tea.

Tich was nursed back to health by Rifleman Walker (a medical
orderly) and would habitually sit next to troops or on the bonnet of
a bren gun carrier or stretcher Jeep. This sight was uplifting for
the men and boosted morale. The King's Royal Rifle troops were
nervous, as any troops are in war time, particularly as the war was
going badly for the Allies at this time. The sight of Tich riding on the
bonnet was naturally uplifting; as bullets and shells began circling
the Corps, Tich did not move from her post, such a sight gave men
confidence and a belief that if a dog was not to be intimidated then
they could stand tall too.

The role of medical orderly Rifleman Walker cannot be dis-
counted. As an orderly his wartime role was one of extreme danger
and stress. As men were wounded and killed his role was to

administer medical attention, and bring men back to the safety of a hospital. Rifleman Walker played a leading part in the rescue, under heavy shelling, of wounded Gurkhas, and Tich, perched on the bonnet of his Jeep, never left her post. When the regimental aid post on the River Marzeno was partially demolished by shell fire, Rifleman Walker took charge with Tich by his side, remaining there throughout. Tich was wounded in the head as the injured men were evacuated out of the hospital and supplies moved to a safer place. The next day Tich led her master through heavy shelling to locate injured troops. Some days later the Corps was required to dig a temporary trench across a battlefield as the regiment came under heavy fire again. As Rifleman Walker and the other troops used shovels, Tich used her claws to dig into the hard African soil for safety.

Lieutenant Colonel Williams recommended Tich for the Dickin Medal and the citation stated:

Her courage and devotion to duty were of very real and considerable value, and her courageous example helped many men to keep their heads and sense of proportion in times of extreme danger. The sight of her put heart into the men as she habitually rode on the bonnet of her master's Jeep and refused to leave her post even when bringing in the wounded under heavy fire.

During conflict at Faneza, in northern Italy, Tich was severly injured as shrapnel from a shell peppered Rifleman Walker's Jeep. With Tich resting on the bonnet she suffered very badly. Her nose was broken and her body was cut badly from several shards of metal. The unit's medical officer declared Tich 'a gonner' but Rifleman Walker nursed her back to health. Tich was then smuggled aboard a ship taking the corps to Italy and *en route* gave birth to a litter of puppies. It took the men of the Corps some considerable skill to keep this hidden from their superiors but they managed and Tich continued to serve in Europe. The Battalion's Chaplain said of Tich, 'She can leap onto any type of truck or vehicle, will howl like a wolf, will cry, will remain standing against a wall until told to move. She will also smoke cigarettes, and never eat or drink until ordered to do so by her owner.' On top of these talents Tich also gave birth to thirty-seven puppies during the war years.

Rifleman Walker earned the Military Medal for his extreme bravery saving lives during the war. Tich was awarded the Dickin Medal for her bravery and devotion to the men in the King's Royal Rifle Corps. After the war ended Thomas Walker returned to Newcastle to run his fruit 'n' veg stall with an extra employee. Tich remained by his side every day with the exception of occasions when her master went to the pub, then Tich would remain outside.

Tich passed away in 1959 and was buried in the PDSA cemetery for Dickin Medal winners at Ilford in Essex. The care and food the men of the Rifle Corps gave Tich was returned many times over and consequentially saved many lives. Tich was awarded the 53rd Dickin Medal.

Paddy
Normandy, 1944

Paddy is the only Irish creature to win the Dickin Medal. Bred in County Antrim, he displayed great speed as a carrier pigeon. Paddy was offered to the Air/Sea Rescue by his owner, Mr Hughes, and began completing flights from the RAF station in Northern Ireland from May 1943 to March 1944. Paddy's speed and consistency was noticed by Sergeant MacLean who was gathering the best carrier pigeons to take part in the D-Day landings in Normandy and was determined to select only the very best. MacLean was confident of Paddy's ability as he had a secret weapon; Paddy's 'wife'.

Pigeons mate for life and Paddy's flight times increased when he shared a loft with his wife who was a 'home bird' and rarely entered races, preferring to remain in the loft to look after her young. Sergeant MacLean took the wise decision to take both Paddy and his wife to the south coast of England to ensure he would perform at his best. After Paddy had completed several flights from RAF stations in the south of England, MacLean, who was in charge of training, considered him to be the best bird in the batch and he was given the code NPS.43.9451.

Each unit in the Normandy landings had a pigeon with them in a wooden cage. There were hundreds of pigeons involved in the landings and most of them were used to relay details of the mission back to England. Paddy was released deep inside Normandy and had to fly 230 miles to reach his loft. Remarkably, of all the pigeons during this mission, he completed this journey in the best recorded time (four hours and five minutes). For this feat he was awarded the Dickin Medal.

After the war had ended, Paddy was returned to Mr Hughes by the RAF Pigeon Service and was given a long rest whilst also siring many outstanding pigeons up to 1954. In May 1954 Mr Hughes allowed his birds to have an open loft with the birds sunning them-selves on the grass in front of the loft after a bath but suddenly, a peregrine falcon swooped over the garden, scaring the birds who flew wildly into the air. Paddy and several other birds flew into electrical wires and he dropped to the ground with a broken neck. A sad end for a brave and extremely fast bird.

Gander
Hong Kong, 1941

In Newfoundland, Canada, in the summer of 1940 a group of children dashed to play with a big dog named Pal who was sitting on a lawn. Newfoundland dogs are large, friendly, calm animals and there have been many tales of heroic rescues from sinking ships or saving children stranded in lakes. Pal was well-known throughout the area as a kind animal and very gentle with children, often pulling sledges in winter and playing with the children during the long summer afternoons. As the children gathered around Pal he put out a paw and scratched the face of a six-year-old girl. This was out of character for Pal. The police were called and Rod Hayden, his owner, feared that Pal may have to be put down. Fate intervened and the 1st Battalion of Royal Rifles stationed in the local town was looking for a mascot for the regiment. Pal was smuggled out to the garrison at night and the men adopted him and renamed him Gander, after the town they were defending.

Shortly afterwards the Royal Rifles were dispatched along with other Commonwealth troops to Hong Kong Island to defend it from Japanese attack. Gander went too. Throughout the battles for Hong Kong, Gander continued to display courage and bravery. In the Battle of Lye Mun, Japanese troops outnumbered the Royal Rifles and began to seize control of a stretch of the beach where they had landed. As the Japanese pushed inland, Gander ran toward them barking and biting those who tried to grab him. This gave the Canadian Royal Rifles time to retreat and regroup. Later, in the same battle, Gander came to the rescue of injured men as the Japanese again made advances. They were approaching wounded men who were sure to be captured or even killed. Gander stood between the men and the advancing Japanese and began barking ferociously and charging at them. Strangely, they did not shoot Gander but changed the direction of approach, giving the angry dog a wide birth. Gander had saved many lives.

Gander's most famous act of bravery came soon after. During a fire fight the Japanese threw a hand grenade into a trench the Rifles were defending. Before anyone could react, Gander seized the grenade in his mouth and ran out of the trench to remove the danger, again saving many lives. Sadly, before Gander could put the grenade down it exploded in his mouth, killing him instantly. His citation reads:

For saving the lives of Canadian infantrymen during the Battle of Lye Mun on Hong Kong Island in December 1941. On 3 documented occasions Pal, aka Gander, the Newfoundland mascot of the Royal Rifles of Canada, engaged the enemy as his regiment joined the Winnipeg Grenadiers, members of Battalion Headquarters 'C' Force and other Commonwealth troops in their courageous defence of the Island. Twice Gander's attacks halted the enemy's advance and protected groups of wounded soldiers. In a final act of bravery the war dog was killed in action gathering a grenade. Without Gander's intervention many more lives would have been lost in the assault.

This story was largely forgotten until a chance discussion in Gander, Newfoundland, between two residents. Mrs Eileen Elms had known the dog as Pal before he joined the Rifles and it was her sister that was scratched by Gander in the summer of 1940. She casually mentioned the story to a local historian named Frank Tibbo. Through their efforts the story of Gander was revived and the Canadian War Museum picked up the trail by recommending Gander for a posthumous Dickin Medal. The recommendation was successful and the award was made on 15 August 2000.

Antis

Europe and North Africa, 1940–45

You have had many adventures by land and by air, and if you have not been in a naval battle it is only because you have not had the opportunity. You have been in action a great many times, and have been wounded, and you have inspired others by your courage and steadfastness on many occasion.

Field Marshall, the Earl Wavell

The Sudetenland, a large chunk of Czechoslovakia, was given away to Hitler's Nazi Germany in 1938. Some months later, Hitler seized the remainder by force. A young Czech man named Robert Vaclav Bozdech decided to flee the country and fight for its freedom.

Robert joined the French Foreign Legion. However, before completing his training France declared war on Germany so he immediately transferred to the French Air Force and trained as a pilot. Soon afterwards he was shot down. He survived the accident but had to begin the long walk through 'no-man's-land' back toward French lines. As he crossed fields he saw a farm and decided to walk in that direction hoping to hitch a lift and, hopefully, find some food. The farm was deserted but as he walked through the damaged buildings he heard a whining. He followed the noise and saw a small Alsatian puppy cowering in the corner of a barn. Robert called out but no-one replied. Robert patted the animal and decided to take him back to the barracks, once there he decided to name him 'Ant' after the Russian planes he had been flying in.

Despite the best efforts of Robert and other Czech airmen, France fell to Germany and the armistice was signed on 22 June 1940. This agreement made Robert and all Czech airmen traitors as Hitler considered them German citizens. For the second time he had to flee, he decided to go south and hoped to reach Algiers. Robert was captured before reaching Algiers and was placed aboard an Italian convoy with Ant. While aboard the ship the entire convoy was sunk by the Royal Navy off the coast of North Africa. The pair were rescued from the sea (Robert swimming with Ant holding onto his shoulders). Upon reaching England he enlisted in the RAF. Given the rank of Aircraftsman, Robert was taken to Cholmondeley near

Liverpool. His English began to improve and Robert learned that his pronunciation of Ant sounded like the English 'Aunt' so his puppy became 'Antis'. Antis loved life on an RAF base and spent his days freely wandering the grounds, being fed from the canteen and making friends with the nurses while his master attended training.

Robert used to walk Antis in the evenings and was joined by a nurse from the medical ward. She invited him to her parents' home in the centre of Liverpool for the weekend. After dinner he decided to walk Antis into the centre of the city and stumbled into a fellow Czech named Stetka. As they walked home together, after visiting a pub, German bombers began to drop their cargo on the city below. Stetka and Bozdech flattened themselves on the pavement and pulled Antis to the ground. Explosions and fires broke out in the surrounding streets, as suddenly as the raid began it stopped. Civil Defence rescue teams arrived on the scene and began to scramble over the wreckage that, minutes earlier, had been terraced housing. One of them screamed at Robert. Despite his limited English the message was understood. The man wanted Antis to search and locate those buried in the rubble of their houses. Robert did not have time to explain that Antis was not trained for such rescue work, but this was not the time to argue. Antis was pulling hard at his leash. After Robert undid his tie, Antis ran toward the bombsite.

Torches pierced the darkness, following Antis's movements. Then he stopped and began scratching at the ground. The men of the rescue party joined in, as did Robert and Stetka. A woman was pulled out of the rubble alive and well but shaken. Antis set off again and four people had been rescued when, without warning a large interior wall collapsed around them, Robert called out for his puppy but there was no reply. Then he heard a loud bark, Robert called Antis to heel but he would not come, so Robert moved over the debris toward the barking, which became increasingly desperate. When he reached Antis he feared the dog was injured but he was standing on all fours, next to him there was a woman holding a small baby, both were partially buried. Immediately Robert called the others and they began to help the casualties. Sadly it was not enough, both died before reaching hospital.

The puppy was lauded as a hero on return to the barracks and was rewarded with extra rations from the canteen. It did not last.

Robert was to be transferred to RAF Honnington. Upon arriving he was told dogs were not welcome in the barracks. Robert refused to give up Antis and set about finding somewhere else to live. An old disused hut, with no heating, became home for the Czech airman and his dog in December 1940. It did have one advantage, the men could be punished with demotion if they were caught drinking in the barracks but as Robert was in a disused hut he could drink freely. On Christmas Day 1940 Robert collected his Christmas dinner and Antis's rations and went back to his hut. After they had finished Stetka and Josef – fellow airmen – visited with several bottles of whiskey. The men drank freely and Antis began to join in, moving happily from glass to glass until he could take no more and slumped down on the floor snoring loudly. The following morning Robert was much the worse for wear. He had great difficulty waking Antis for his morning walk, but when he managed to rise Antis went straight to the fire station buckets and drained the water. After his thirst was quenched he was in tip top order and happy to start his walk.

Throughout this period Robert continued to serve on bombing sorties over Europe in 311 Squadron. When Robert was away Antis used to sit and wait on the airfield with the ground crew for his master to return. One of the crew, Adamek, noticed that he would rise to all fours before Robert's plane was visible, Antis could detect his master's plane by the hum of the engine despite there being many planes coming into land. On 12 June Robert's plane came under heavy enemy fire on a bombing raid, the engine malfunctioned and Robert was struck in the head by shrapnel. The stricken plane slumped gently toward the waves of the channel as it tried to reach home, the crew managed to land at RAF Coltishall, Robert was taken to hospital in Norwich.

Antis sat waiting for his master's return. He did not sit up as the bombers returned, and even after the final bomber landed he refused to go inside, growling at anyone who tried to move him. Robert was attended to and sent a telegram to the ground crew asking them to take care of Antis for a few days but no-one could get the dog inside. For two days and nights Antis remained next to the runway staring into the sky above. Robert discharged himself and hitched a lift to his airbase. Once there he went straight to the runway, Antis immediately jumped up and ran toward him barking wildly.

After a period of rehabilitation Robert resumed duty. A few weeks later, on a bombing raid over Bremen, the captain began to struggle with the controls of the plane; ice was gathering on the wings. Worse news followed as an electrical storm broke out, lightning struck the bomber and all the instruments and radio failed. Robert felt something touch his elbow. Expecting to see a crew member Robert turned around and saw Antis. He did not look well, they were thousands of feet in the air with little oxygen. Robert took off his breathing mask and placed it on Antis' nose, after several deep breaths Robert informed the captain of the stowaway. With no working instruments the crew decided not to continue with the raid, they turned for home and landed with no further problems. Upon landing the crew viewed the presence of Antis as a good omen and decided they would take him on all missions. Although they often wondered how he managed to get aboard that first flight.

Antis had a special oxygen mask made for him with a container; he would lie on the floor of the plane and sleep or simply watch the crew go about their work. On a later raid shrapnel exploded near the aircraft and pierced the mask, it struck Antis in the face and his left ear. Upon landing he received medical attention after completing his victory lap of the plane, but his left ear continued to droop.

The next raid in the newly-christened aircraft 'Cecelia' was much more severe. Above Mannheim she came under fierce attack, a shell exploded under her belly and Cecelia nearly somersaulted, shrapnel sprayed through her body piercing the fuselage. Hot oil splattered the cockpit and a huge gaping hole emerged in the floor between the pilots. The crew was unhurt but next came the searchlights from below, Cecelia was struggling to escape the glare, her controls were sluggish as she juddered forward; she was a sitting duck. Fighter planes could be heard swarming nearby; Robert expected his next moment to be his last, he bent down to pat Antis on the head.

Cecelia limped on; the expected fighter assault did not come and she throbbed her way toward a mass of thick cloud and safety. When Robert felt safe he looked down at Antis. He remained still and calm. Too still. Robert shone a torch on his dog and saw a pool of thick blood. Antis had been lying on the floor that had been raked with shrapnel; he was hit in the stomach and had lost a lot of blood. Antis had not called out for help or distracted any of the crew as they battled against the enemy. Upon landing Cecelia had not reached a complete stop when Robert jumped out with Antis in his arms; he was taken to the medical ward. Antis recovered, but his flying days were over.

On 1 September 1941 Robert Vaclav Bozdech was awarded the Czechoslovak Medal for Valour and promoted to flight sergeant. Whilst away on training Antis was looked after by fellow airmen. One day Robert received a call from Vladimir who had walked him the previous day. Antis had broken away, jumped into a farmers' field and chased after some sheep. Before Vladimir could catch up with him the farmer had fired his shotgun, Antis was hit, but not seriously hurt. However the offence of chasing sheep was severe, food was scarce in wartime and farmers were permitted to shoot any dogs scaring sheep. Magistrates had instructed that many dogs be put down. The farmer noted the description of Antis and Vladimir's rank and number, the police were informed and Antis was summoned to appear before Cowbridge magistrates on 3 March 1942. Robert was worried, and with good reason.

Despite appealing to his commanding officers Robert was not granted permission to leave his training to attend court. Vladimir took Antis and promised to speak on Robert's behalf. The local police requested the court to grant an order for Antis to be put to sleep. The evidence and mitigation was produced, Antis's complete war record was read out in court listing thirty-two operational flights including injuries sustained in the line of duty. Vladimir explained how the quick return of Antis safe and sound would be appreciated as the squadron considered the dog to be a lucky omen. The magistrates decided to fine Vladimir eleven shillings and ordered that Antis should be returned to his owner but kept under strict control. Antis was free.

A reporter was present in court and listened to the story of Antis with interest, a few days later the headline 'Dog went with RAF on Raids' appeared in the *Sunday Mail*, whilst the *South Wales Echo* had a front page article entitled, 'Dog that flies over Germany – His Life Spared for more trips!'. Antis became a celebrity and news of his exploits became a morale boost for many people fighting a difficult war. Robert decided to train Antis to resist the urge to chase sheep and with the co-operation of a local farmer he practised for hours in the evening by releasing Antis from his lead in a field full of sheep, Antis was a quick learner and after two weeks conquered his urge.

Robert was transferred to Scotland but news of his dog had reached northern Britain and Antis was afforded the run of the RAF base. So much so that when Robert patted Antis goodbye and boarded a bus to the local town for a dance, Antis simply waited for the next bus and boarded it to follow his master. He ended up miles away in Inverness. Fortunately a Czech airman recognised him and sent a telegram informing Robert that Antis could have a place on a training flight back to RAF Evanton. Robert decided to take Antis along to some social events, but petrol was rationed so it was often hard to get to dances in the sparse Scottish environment. Some Czech servicemen clubbed together and bought a car but instead of using petrol they managed to set up a second fuel system using aviation fuel. Locals were surprised to see the same vehicle at most pubs and parties in the area and often commented on its speed and the strange odour left in its wake.

After long years of fighting, eventually Germany was defeated. Robert and Antis were demobbed and free to return to Czechoslovakia. On 13 August 1945 they flew home to Prague. People in Czechoslovakia did not know about their countrymen fighting with the Allies. The first time they saw these men came during the Victory Parade through the streets of the capital city, a parade in which both Robert and Antis took part. Antis was used to noise and crowds after years on RAF bases and he loved the celebrations as they moved through the cobbled streets. A woman ran up to Robert and kissed him passionately.

After the celebrations had died down Robert was made a Captain and Antis an official war dog. Both continued to serve but now they were enlisted in the Czech Air Force at Rozyn. In November 1945 he met Tatiana Zilka at a ball, they married two months later. They had met before, she was the woman who had kissed Robert at the Victory Parade in Prague. Antis was not allowed into the church for the ceremony but got so excited as they emerged man and wife that he got entangled in the bride's train. Robert's friend, Doctor Jan Masaryk, a prominent politician, gave the couple an apartment in

1. Winkie, with the crew she saved from the North Sea. (*Courtesy of the Imperial War Museum*)

2. Jet of Iada, proudly displaying his Animal VC.

3. Rob's collar and Dickin Medal. Rob was the eleventh winner of the Animal VC. (*Courtesy of Miss Heather Bayne*)

TO THE DEAR MEMORY OF ROB
WAR DOG Nº 471/322 TWICE V.C.
BRITAINS FIRST PARACHUTE DOG
WHO SERVED 3½ YEARS IN
NORTH AFRICA AND ITALY WITH THE
2ND SPECIAL AIR SERVICE REGT.
DIED 18TH JAN. 1952
AGED 12½ YEARS.

ERECTED BY BASIL AND HEATHER BAYNE
IN MEMORY OF A FAITHFUL FRIEND
AND PLAYMATE.

1939   1952

4. Rob's gravestone at the home of Miss Heather Bayne in Ellesmere. (*Courtesy of Miss Heather Bayne*)

Any further communication on
this subject should be addressed
to—
The Under-Secretary of State,
The War Office
(as opposite),
and the following number quoted.

B.M. 593/2 (V&R)

Your Reference

THE WAR OFFICE,
Droitwich Spa,
Worcestershire.

24th January, 1945.

Sir,

I am directed to inform you that it is proposed to award the "Dickin" medal for Gallantry to War Dog No. 471/322, "Rob", which you were good enough to loan for War Service on the 19th May, 1942.

Since the dog has been with the Armed Forces he has given invaluable service, and it is hoped that you will agree to this presentation to commemorate his conspicuous devotion to duty.

Subject to your approval, it is hoped that the medal will be awarded on the 8th February, 1945, and I should be grateful if you would kindly confirm that you are agreeable to this presentation. A pre-paid envelope is attached for your convenience in replying.

May I take this opportunity of again expressing our appreciation of your patriotic gesture in loaning "Rob" for service.

I am, Sir,
Your obedient Servant,

J. C. Bennison

Lieut.Colonel, for,
Brigadier,
Director,
Army Veterinary and Remount Services.

E. Bayne, Esq.,
Laurel House,
Tetehill,
Ellesmere,   SALOP.

5. The letter from the War Office informing the Bayne family of Rob's Dickin Medal award from the PDSA. (*Courtesy of Miss Heather Bayne*)

6. Rip helps unearth a victim of the Blitz whilst his handler, Mr King, looks on. (*Courtesy of the Imperial War Museum*)

7. Buster, winner of the Animal VC for detecting a hoard of terrorist ammunition, with his handler, Sergeant Danny Morgan. (*Courtesy of Corbis Images*)

8. Rifleman Khan with his handler, Corporal Muldoon, whom he rescued from drowning during the attack on Walcheren in 1944. (*Courtesy of the Imperial War Museum*)

9. DD43T139 is released by the crew of a stricken ship off the coast of New Guinea. (*Elizabeth Keen*)

10. A soldier releases William of Orange into the air. (*Elizabeth Keen*)

11. Judy, the only animal registered as a prisoner of war who returned from captivity to have her bark recorded on BBC radio. (*Courtesy of the Imperial War Museum*)

12. Two Dickin Medal winners; Mr Bill Barnett holds Beauty aloft (right) and Irma stands with her handler, Mrs Margaret Griffin who was later awarded the British Empire Medal for her work training rescue dogs. (*Courtesy of the Imperial War Museum*)

13. Ricky, a Welsh Sheepdog, suffered head injuries and damaged hearing after a mine exploded killing his commander, but he managed to help the remaining men to safety. (*Courtesy of the Imperial War Museum*)

central Prague. Robert and Tatiana settled into married life and they had a son.

Domestic life for Robert did not last. In 1948 democracy in Czechoslovakia was extinguished. A Communist coup behind the façade of free elections seized control on 27 February. The Communist Prime Minister Klement Gottwald used trade union police and the militia to force the formation of a new cabinet. The hopes of those who opposed communism rested with Dr Jan Masaryk, who retained his post as Foreign Minister.

On 10 March 1948 Masaryk was found dead in the courtyard of the Foreign Ministry in Prague. Still dressed in his pyjamas, the official enquiry stated Masaryk had committed suicide by jumping from the window of his apartment on the first floor. Rumours circulated the city of scratches visible on the ledge of the window and stone fragments underneath Masaryk's fingernails. Masaryk had also been planning his upcoming wedding to an American author. The new Communist government, inspired by Stalinist principles began to hunt down those who believed in, and fought for democracy. Robert knew he did not have much time, Masaryk himself had warned Robert that his name was on a 'hit list'. He decided to flee for freedom, nine years after he first left Czechoslovakia. It would not be easy, the borders were patrolled by a new breed of zealous Communist guards who thought nothing of firing on fellow Czechs if it meant promotion in the Communist government. Trains and aerodromes would not offer a chance of escape as routes to the free world were cut off. The target was the American controlled part of West Germany, Robert decided he would make his way through Bohemia to the village of Furth-Im-Wald, then cross the border on foot.

The journey was fraught with danger. Many Czech nationals were intent on escaping their homeland in search of the freedom they had fought so hard to regain in the war. Nevertheless, Robert decided to go through with his plan, he agreed to go with two other men named Anton and Franka. Anton was an officer in the Czech Air Force and Franka a young man of eighteen who initially drove the others part of the way but decided to join the escape at the last minute. Robert, of course, took Antis with him and booked a few days leave to give himself a head start before anyone realised that he was missing. Robert decided that he would not tell Tatiana of his decision to flee. He felt that she would understand his decision, but also that when the Communist officials interrogated her she would be better not knowing where he had gone. Robert and his party managed to reach the outskirts of Furth-Im-Wald, on the border. It was still light so they lay low in woods until nightfall. The route on foot would be difficult with thick woodland, rivers and mountains. The border guards had a shoot-on-sight policy. As night fell Robert set Antis to work, he led the three men through the dense woods, and each man understood that one mistake could lead to the death of the others.

Antis would remain by Robert's side as they moved through the trees but when a clearing appeared Robert released Antis to investigate. Guards armed with rifles and machine guns roamed the area. They had dogs too. Sometimes Antis would disappear for a few seconds before returning and leading the men across the open ground. At other times it seemed like hours before he reappeared next to Robert. It was slow progress. After three hours the men reached a valley with a river flowing through it, on the other side of the river was the border with West Germany.

The lives of the three men were in the hands of Antis. The men rested at the edge of the woods and Robert noticed Antis staring intently at a copse a short distance away. When he placed his hand on his back he could feel his dog tense his muscles. Each man feared that a guard was hiding in the bushes so they pressed themselves to the ground; from the bushes emerged a deer. Without warning Antis raced into the clearing running through the long grass toward the deer, Robert's first instinct was to call Antis to heel as he had done in the field full of sheep, but that would alert the guards. The three men, flat to the ground, watched as Antis continued to run but then, Antis stopped in his tracks. Half covered by the long grass, he remained still as the deer grazed ahead of him. Antis then turned and sloped back toward the men, when he reached Robert, Antis received a pat from Robert's trembling hand. The deer moved away, the men relaxed.

Antis then led the men slowly through the valley toward the river. Half way between the river and the line of trees Antis, without warning, dropped to the ground. Robert, Anton and Franka did the same. Robert touched Antis, his dog was rigid with tension. In the moonlight, through the long grass Robert could see that it was too far to move back toward the safety of the trees. Out of the darkness, Robert then heard voices. The men, fearing that guards were right on top of them did not move. The voices came nearer, he could feel Antis rising as if to challenge the advancing party, Robert pushed his body against his dog and Antis remained pressed against the grass. Slowly the voices became louder, Robert was unsure if it was a group of fellow escapees or guards moving back to the border. The voices drew level with Antis and the men, but the advancing party did not stop and moved on toward the river.

After a few minutes Antis relaxed and rose to his feet, Robert, Anton and Franka did the same. The next moment the silence was broken by a volley of machine gun fire accompanied by searchlights and shouting from across the river, beams of light swung violently across the valley. Without warning the gunfire stopped and the valley went quiet. As the border guards moved across a small bridge to gain a closer look at the men they had just killed, a car pulled up and two officers stepped out. Guards stood laughing, as if pleased with their kill, and a lorry pulled up as the searchlights continued to light up valley. The bodies were loaded aboard. The searchlights were switched off and silence fell once more across the valley.

Robert peered through the blades of long grass and saw the lorry drive away. The group that had passed Robert, Anton, Franka and Antis moments earlier as they lay on the grass had been gunned down attempting to reach freedom; it could so easily have been them. Antis's warning had delayed them, as they lost themselves in the long grass, others had moved toward the border and paid with their lives. Antis did not relax, Robert feared a patrol would be sent up the valley to find more escapees. Robert decided to move back toward the line of trees and safety. Once there, the men decided that to attempt crossing into West Germany in the valley was suicidal so they hatched a new plan.

Franka knew the region well and advised that the best option was a long trek through dense woods to the foot of a peak, where the river could be crossed as it meandered around the hill. Once across the river they could scale the hill and make their way down the other side, across some fields and into West Germany. Franka believed the area was lightly guarded as few would dare to edge down the craggy rocks at night. There would still be wire fences and some guards. It would also take most of what remained of the night but it was safer.

Again Antis led the men through the woods until, at last, a craggy rock appeared. Robert could hear the river trickling but, in the darkness, they could not see where it was best to cross. In the pitch black the men held hands, with Robert at the rear clenching Antis's collar, and slipped quietly into the river. It was icy cold and waste-deep, the current was too powerful and Robert not only lost his grip on Anton's hand but also on Antis' collar. Using his free hands to steady himself and scramble through the water Robert managed to reach the other side of the river. Soaking wet and very cold Robert looked around him but could not see or hear anyone. For a split second he thought of calling for Antis but realised this may alert guards in the area and stopped himself. There was only one option, wait for Antis to find him before the border guards did.

It was only minutes later that Robert felt Antis next to him, he then set his dog to work rounding up Anton and Franka. Antis returned quickly with Franka but then disappeared for some time. He finally returned with Anton who explained that the current had swept him downstream. Antis had found him next to a river bank and guided him through the rocks and trees. The men looked up at the hill in front of them and considered moving around the contours, which would be slower. It was now 1.00 am and they decided to scale the peak. It soon proved to be a mistake. Scrambling up rock, uneven ground and thick undergrowth was difficult but soon a thick mist descended on them, they were climbing as if blind. Upon reaching a point where they could no longer climb the men looked down on the other side of the hill, but could see nothing of what lay ahead. Attempting a descent was too dangerous so the men huddled together for warmth on a ledge. Robert whispered words of praise into the ear of Antis.

Two hours had passed and the mist had gradually cleared. Each man moved across the peak looking for a suitable way down, and left Antis on the ledge. After deciding on a suitable path down, the men walked back up to collect Antis but as they neared the ledge they heard the sound of falling rocks and a scuffle. Robert ran toward the ledge, fearing Antis had tried to come after them and fallen. When the men reached the ledge they found Antis in a vicious rage growling at a guard he had pinned to the ground, Antis was a big dog and Robert had never seen such anger radiating from him. They quickly disarmed the guard, tying him to a tree and gagging him before beginning their descent to freedom.

They moved quickly and after thirty minutes they had reached the bottom, West Germany was in sight. Robert could see a small river to cross and some open arable land with a line of stones running across it marking the border. But there was also a small wooden hut with some sandbags and two telephone wires, it was the post of the guard they had left tied to a tree on the mountainside. Nervously the men whispered to each other, wondering if the guard was alone on duty. The open arable land was visible from the guard post. The men could not afford to be seen as they crossed the border so, reluctantly and with a heavy heart, Robert sent Antis toward the hut.

Silently Antis walked toward the hut, he sniffed the door then scratched at it as Robert, Anton and Franka watched from the trees. No answer came, the men sprinted toward the hut, collecting Antis on the way, and jumped into the small stream. Dripping wet they then crossed the fields and the row of stones into West Germany and freedom; they had made it.

Stumbling across a small town the men presented themselves at a local police station and claimed asylum. After surrendering their weapons the party was taken to the US Air Force Base at Straubing. It was from here that Robert met other refugees and learned of Tatiana's fate. After Robert failed to report for duty Communist officials appeared at his apartment and questioned Tatiana. They did not take her away for interrogation and she safely moved to her parents' home with their son. Tatiana unfortunately had a difficult time in the new Communist Republic; she was 'tainted' by marriage to Robert and would, time and again, be hounded out of employment by government officials until, years later, she finally agreed to divorce Robert. The date of the separation was backdated to 27 February 1948. Robert would not learn of his divorce until years later.

Robert moved to England, his adopted country but upon arrival he was told Antis would have to be held in quarantine for six months. Antis was held at Hackbridge and Robert, who rejoined the RAF, visited him on Wednesdays and Saturdays. But in October 1948 Robert was injured in a training exercise, breaking his leg, which was set in plaster after admission to Innsworth Hospital, preventing him from visiting Antis. Robert was worried, he remembered sustaining shrapnel wounds during the war when Antis refused to leave the air field until he returned. His loyalty to his master had brought him near death. Robert tried to persuade the Medical Officer to allow him to travel but Robert was not well enough for such a journey.

On 11 November Robert was admitted to the Collaton Cross Military Unit near Plymouth, his but still his doctors would not allow him to travel to visit Antis. After two weeks Robert opened a letter from the vets at Hackbridge kennels. Fearing the worst he opened it to discover Antis had stopped eating, was gravely ill and likely to die soon. Robert took the letter to his Medical Officer, who remembered reading of Antis during the war, and agreed to transfer him to a medical unit in Surrey. Upon being transferred Robert made the short trip to Hackbridge.

The staff spoke to Robert before he saw Antis, and prepared him for the worst. When Robert saw Antis he was lying motionless with little sign of life. There was no response when Robert called out his name. Robert cupped his head and talked to him; Antis responded and after half an hour lapped up a bowl of milk. Visiting time ended, to show Antis he would return, Robert left his gloves beside his bed. Robert left the kennels deeply upset. In a short time he had lost his freedom, family and country. Antis was all he had. On his way back to the medical unit Robert noticed a church, he went in and prayed. The next day Robert returned to the kennels, Antis had improved. Despite the vet's warning that his age would make a full recovery difficult, Antis continued to get better as Robert visited him each day until, in January 1949, the quarantine period ended. Antis joined Robert on his RAF base and was quickly back to his old self, so much so that when Robert spent the weekend with friends Antis lay across the doorway to his guest bedroom and snarled at anyone trying to enter, even the lady of the house who wished to change the bed sheets.

Shortly afterwards, Antis was recommended for the Animal Victoria Cross and received his medal at Earls Court on 28 January 1949 from the PDSA. The citation read:

> *Owned by a Czech airman, this dog served with him in the French Air Force and RAF from 1940 to 1945, both in North Africa and England. Returning to Czechoslovakia after the war, he substantially helped his master's escape across the frontier when, after the death of Jan Masaryk, he had to fly from the Communists.*

Robert continued his career in the RAF and was restored to his wartime rank of Flight Sergeant. On 22 June 1951 he became a British citizen. He was transferred to Scotland and Antis continued to enjoy life on the base, wandering around during the day and being well-fed by the canteen cook. However, the harsh winter of 1952/3 took its toll on Antis, the battle scars and short absences from Robert next to the runway at Honnington and in Hackbridge had weakened him. As Robert lay on his bed in the barracks he felt Antis lie heavily on his chest, when ordered to his bed Antis did not move. Slowly Antis rose to his feet, clambered down from the bunk toward his bed on the floor but collapsed before reaching his bed.

The next morning it was clear Antis was unwell. He had lost the strength in his legs and would not eat much. Robert took him to the local vet, who advised putting Antis to sleep. Robert sat in his barracks, looked at the pictures of his family arranged next to his bunk, the family in Czechoslovakia that was cut off from contact. Robert found it hard to decide what to do, Antis was his only link to home, so he wrote to the PDSA for advice. A telegram reply said:

> *Advise putting old friend out of misery. Grave reserved.*

Robert made the arrangements for the following morning. That evening he walked with Antis for the final time. In the morning they travelled to Ilford, the PDSA headquarters. Antis was placed on the surgeon's table, his body was weak and his left ear still drooped but his eyes still displayed a sharp alertness. Robert held his beloved dog, tears rolling down his face, as the surgeon gently put Antis to sleep.

Antis died on 11 August 1953 and is buried at the PDSA cemetery at Ilford. He was fourteen years old. The inscription on his gravestone reads:

> *There is an old belief,*
> *That on some solemn shore*
> *Beyond the sphere of grief,*
> *Dear friends shall meet once more.*

Underneath reads a Czech phrase *'Verny Az Do Smrti'* which means 'Loyal unto Death'.

Princess
Egypt, 1943

Some animals in this book displayed great courage and determination during most, if not throughout the war years, and others completed numerous missions involving extreme danger. Princess was a smoky blue hen pigeon of Egyptian origin and was given one very special but extremely difficult mission.

Trained by the RAF at a station in Alexandria, Princess was selected for a mission whereby the information that was to be transported was extremely valuable. Even today I have been unable to locate the exact information due to its secrecy, or even who the agent was that accompanied Princess. As intelligence agents are never discarded by government agencies, only allowed 'leave' as a method of exerting control over them should they wish to divulge details of their exploits, I doubt we will ever know what was written on the paper tucked into the capsule on the leg of this pigeon.

Nevertheless, in April 1943, Princess was taken to Crete on a mission of importance and was released with the brief to fly to Alexandria, Egypt. This was a distance of 500 miles mostly across open sea. This was especially difficult as Princess would have no opportunity to rest or scavenge for food. Remarkably Princess 'homed' in to the RAF base in Alexandria at 16:30 hrs on the 14 April and this was regarded the finest long distance performance from a member of the National Pigeon Service throughout the war.

As was often the case with heroic animals they were often used in parades and exhibitions to collect funds for the war effort, provide care for injured animals or simply boost morale. Whilst on display in Cairo Princess contracted an infection and died soon afterwards. Sadly, Princess did not live to collect her medal which was awarded in May 1946.

PART 5

HEROES ABROAD

Lucky
Malaysia, 1949–52

Malaya was a colony in the British Empire successfully invaded in 1941 by the Japanese. The British surrendered in February 1942 and the people of Malaya suffered three years of barbaric occupation. The British supported the Malay People's Anti Japanese Army (MPAJA), which was a Communist resistance movement formed to harass the occupying Japanese. In September 1945, the Communists intended to seize power and turn Malaya into a Communist state, but the British Military Administration was very quick to take control and thwarted their aim. Although the MPAJA was disbanded, many of its members simply remained in the jungle with their weapons and equipment. The Malayan Communist Party was still a legal political party, but it was behind many strikes, attacks on rubber planters and their workforce, and the intimidation of the Malayan population, so in June 1948 it was banned. However, the Communists simply moved into the jungle with their weapons, where many of the former MPAJA comrades were still holed up, and they reorganised in preparation for an armed struggle. The newly formed Communist terrorists began a campaign of violence and mines, villages and plantations were attacked, and many civilians were murdered.

A state of emergency was declared and the Coldstream Guards, 2nd Battalion Royal Scots Guards and the Ghurkas were deployed. Among them were four dogs named Bobbie, Jasper, Lassie and Lucky. These forces had two objectives, firstly to prevent the attacks and ensure the safety of the population of Malaya and, secondly, to attack and neutralise the terrorist threat.

Bobbie, Jasper, Lassie and Lucky accompanied the men on patrols to track terrorists in the jungle. Tracking was an especially difficult task in the Malayan jungle because of the searing heat and overgrown vegetation. Lucky was handled by Corporal Bevel Austin Stapleton (Bev) and they were inseparable for the next three years.

On 31 December 1951, Lucky and Bev were on patrol when they came under gunfire from the undergrowth. They were deafened by the shots and could not make out the direction in which the terrorist had made his escape. Lucky set off, quickly followed by Bev and the rest of the patrol, they moved silently through the thick jungle and stopped when Lucky gave the signal that the terrorist was lying a few metres ahead of them. The men surrounded the terrorist and detained him. On 3 February Lucky and Bev were involved in a special operation to flush out the insurgents, organised by the RAF and Civil Police. Air attacks on the terrorists were strategically placed to drive them into ambushes laid by organised patrols.

There were dangers with this work. Lucky and the other patrol dogs were invaluable as they gave an early warning that the enemy was in the vicinity. This often meant the dogs were the first to be seen by insurgents as described by this extract from *RAF Police Dogs on Patrol* by Stephen R. Davies:

> *On the 21 January 1950, Corporals Stapleton and Thackray were called out to assist soldiers of the Green Howard's Regiment in locating a wounded terrorist who had escaped into an area of swamp. As soon as the NCOs had been briefed they set about searching the area with their dogs for a scent to follow. Soon after, two of the dogs, Bobby and Lassie, jumped into a stretch of water and something appeared to go tragically wrong; Bobbie just disappeared below the surface, while Lassie convulsed, bit her back and immediately sank below the water. At that point Corporal Stapleton saw that there were lots of dead fish floating on the surface and then noticed a cable running into the water. A later enquiry established that it was a live electric cable, which had been severed by a bullet and which had dropped into the water. Although both police dogs had been instantly killed by the 30,000 volt current, their loss had actually saved their handlers and other members of the patrol from being electrocuted.*

On another patrol Bev spotted a man's face in the undergrowth and raised the alarm. A firefight began, with a hail of bullets showering the jungle whilst Lucky moved to the area where the man had been seen. Lucky found a rifle and a grenade and continued to follow his scent, with the patrol behind her; they then suddenly saw the man running at speed and opened fire killing him. The man was identified as Lang Jan Sang, a notorious gang leader responsible for the death of many local people.

Throughout the three years from 1949 to 1952, the four dogs provided companionship, protection and leadership for the men in the

Police Corps, 2nd Battalion Royal Scots and the Coldstream Guards. The determination and jungle tracking skills of the four dogs and their two handlers led to the capture of many terrorists thus preventing further casualties. Bobbie, Jasper, Lassie and Lucky all displayed remarkable devotion to duty despite the searing heat and thick undergrowth of the Malayan jungle. Sadly, Lucky was the only animal to survive the conflict and return to Britain.

Many years passed before the PDSA decided to award a Dickin Medal to one of the dogs who served in the Malaya conflict. As there were four animals, a ballot was taken to decide which animal should receive the posthumous award and Lucky was selected. Bev, receiving the medal on behalf of Lucky in recognition of his service in the campaign on 6 February 2007, said he was pleased Lucky's efforts in Malaya had been recognised. He had feared the recognition would never come. Lucky had been his soulmate in the jungle. Bev retired after thirty-six years active service. The citation read:

For outstanding gallantry and devotion to duty of the RAF Police Anti-terrorist Tracker Dog Team, comprising Bobbie, Jasper, Lassie and Lucky, while attached to the Civil Police and several British Army regiments including the Coldstream Guards, 2nd Battalion Royal Scots Guards and the Ghurkas during the Malaya Campaign. Bobbie, Jasper, Lassie and Lucky displayed exceptional determination and life-saving skills. The dogs and their handlers were an exceptional team, capable of tracing and locating the enemy by scent despite the unrelenting heat and an almost impregnable jungle to the end of the conflict.

Ruhr Express
Germany, 1945

During early 1945 the retreating German Army began to gather in the Ruhr valley to organise a counter attack against the advancing Allied forces and defend the borders of the German nation. By March, approximately 400,000 German troops were in the region and the American and British armies planned a final assault to end the Second World War. The Ruhr had been heavily bombed during the past four-and-a-half years as it contained numerous cities and was famed as the industrial heartland of Germany. These soldiers and the Ruhr were protected by two large rivers, the Rhine and the Oder. The defences were very well-fortified and if the allies could make it past the rivers and into the Ruhr they would have access to the north German plain – the main route into Berlin. Such was the success of the river crossings by the British and American armies they were soon encircling the Ruhr valley.

Twenty-one German divisions, along with many civilians, lived in the bombed-out cities where food was scarce. On 4 April the US 1st and 9th Armies surrounded the Ruhr and sent in small groups of paratroopers to gather intelligence reports on the location of German divisions, artillery and the morale of the opposition, before launching the final assault.

Ruhr Express, code NPS.43.29018, was a large dark chequered cock bird with a sheen of green and blue around his neck. He was bred and trained at the RAF Station in Detling. After two-and-a-half years of excellent service and emergency intercommunication, he was selected from the RAF pigeons to accompany a US force on a reconnaissance mission behind enemy lines in the Ruhr. During his service he proved himself to be a crack pigeon with a natural intelligence, completing difficult tasks such as successfully leaving an aeroplane at 1,000 feet and flying down in a small basket. Such was his success, he was used to train other pigeons. For the mission into the Ruhr Valley only the best were selected; paratroopers would drop into the Ruhr Valley and collect detailed information about the location of enemy troops and defensive positions, before attaching the intelligence report to the bird.

The men boarded a flight that took them over the Ruhr. They then parachuted into a forest with Ruhr Express in a small wooden cage. All the men landed safely and the bird was still in his cage as the men set off through the night to observe the German positions and defences. After successfully gathering all the intelligence, the men carefully removed Ruhr Express from the cage and scribbled the details on a scrap of paper before attaching it to the bird's leg, they then encouraged the pigeon to fly off into the night. Ruhr Express was given the task of flying 300 miles, overnight, to his loft across land and sea. This he did in good time and the details that reached headquarters had a direct impact on the invasion of the Ruhr.

With this and other intelligence the allied forces planned the attack, knowing where the majority of enemy soldiers were stationed and how strong the defences were. The Ruhr fell on 18 April, just fourteen days after the allies encircled the region and the surrender came on the 21st. The war in Europe was over and the excellent work by the men who fought for freedom and Ruhr Express helped to end the siege and save many lives on both sides.

Ruhr Express survived the war and attended shows and festivals where crowds flocked to see the feathered war hero. At one of these fairs, the Bethnal pigeon show, he received the Dickin Medal for:

Carrying an important message from the Ruhr Pocket in excellent time, while serving with the RAF in April 1945.

Ruhr Express was afterwards put up for auction at the PDSA show in the grounds of the Royal Hospital in Chelsea to raise money for the RAF Benevolent Fund and the Allied Forces Animals' War Memorial. Bidding crept higher and higher as the shocked crowd watched, eventually Ruhr Express was sold for the princely sum of £420, a lot of money in war torn England at the end of 1945. At the time the fee was a record for a racing pigeon beating the previous record of £225 set in 1925. The new owner used him and a second bird bought on the day, Per Ardua, to start a new strain of long distance flyers. Per Ardua was sent to Gibraltar to serve during 1944 but suffered homesickness and decided to desert. After being cooped up for thirteen days to nest, she was allowed out for her first flight, promptly decided Gibraltar was not for her and flew

1,000 miles back to her loft in Gillingham. Rather than receive punishment for her actions Per Ardua was lauded for a remarkable flying performance; she covered the distance in what, at most, could only have been twelve days, albeit arriving in a state of total exhaustion. This flight beat the previous British record for a 1,000 mile flight by approximately sixteen days. Along with Ruhr Express, Per Ardua went on to produce a large family of great racing pigeons that were renowned for their long distance flying.

William of Orange
Holland, 1944

During 1944 a swift advance was made by Allied forces into France and Belgium; the British Army had progressed at such an astonishing rate that logistical problems began to mount, not least that of communication. Failure to exert continued pressure against the German retreat could have allowed dangerous counter-attacks to develop. With this in mind the British forces decided to continue their advance into Holland to the Zuider Zee, an inlet of water near the North Sea. The last natural frontier to face was the Rhine, this river had to be crossed using one of the few bridges that remained standing.

Lieutenant-General Montgomery devised a bold plan named Operation 'Market Garden', whereby the Allied Airborne Division would gain a decisive foothold on the eastern riverbank of the Rhine. Two American and one British division were to seize strategically important bridges stretching across the smaller rivers to the west of the Rhine, then push on to take the bridge at Arnhem. The success of this mission would enable the Allies to move into central Europe and attack the heart of the German Army. Montgomery was attempting to end the war as early as possible, as a result planning for the campaign was poor. Paratroopers would drop in zones along the road from Eindhoven to Arnhem, and each group would attempt to successfully carry out their mission.

The US 101st Airborne Division would seize the bridge over a canal at Veghel, the US 82nd Airborne Division would attempt to control the bridge at Grave and the British XXX Corps, led by General Horrocks, would attack Arnhem, which included the men from 2 Para who would go straight for the main bridge and try to hold it until reinforcements could arrive. Despite the campaign being hastily put together, it was well supported. On Sunday 17 September an airborne armada set off across southern England, the formation was 16km across and 150km deep. On board alongside paratroopers were Jeeps, trucks, artillery and bridging equipment should the German infantry destroy any bridges. Terrain in this region would be difficult; Arnhem and Oosterbeek were low lying islands with waterlogged land all around.

Intelligence reports suggested that resistance would be minimal, consisting mostly of old men, brainwashed Hitler youth and Dutch troops who could not wait to change sides and join the Allies. However, for reasons that have still not come to light, British intelligence lost the location of the veteran 9th and 10th SS Panzer Divisions, which had moved up to the Arnhem region. One of the British Horsa gliders crashed whilst dropping men and equipment, this had disastrous results as the Germans managed to rescue a set of battle plans for Market Garden. Armed with this information the SS Panzer tank divisions attacked the Allied paratroopers all along the road to Arnhem to such an extent it was given the nickname 'Hell's Highway'.

Accompanying the men of 2 Para was a pigeon named William of Orange. Sir William Proctor Smith of Bexton House near Knutsford in Cheshire, bred William in 1942 and he was the twenty-first animal to win the Dickin Medal. A handsome mealy cock, William displayed a great aptitude for speed during training with MI14, the agency specialising in German intelligence, and once flew 68 miles in just fifty-nine minutes. Blessed with such astonishing speed, William was soon noticed and he was specially selected to accompany 2 Para to Arnhem. Commanded by Major John Frost, 2 Para had managed to reach the bridge at Arnhem and, despite fierce resistance from the SS, seized one. Unfortunately the divisional commander, Major-General Urquhart, was not aware of this news as the radio equipment was not working. On the bridge the battle was intense and the men of 2 Para group desperately needed reinforcements but they were ordered to hold the area for four days, they clung to their positions for nine but the situation grew increasingly desperate.

The unexpected appearance of the 9th and 10th SS Panzer Divisions prevented XXX Corps reaching the Arnhem road bridge. The small band of men continued to defend the bridge but eventually they were overwhelmed by a fierce counter-attack by the Panzer divisions. German forces counter attacked and encircled 2 Para who were cut off from the main group, after the order to retreat to the higher ground west of Oosterbeek failed to get through. A gunfight ensued and the men were pinned down by constant fire, communications in the battle were poor and the few remaining radio sets malfunctioned. Lacking heavy weapons, short of food, water, ammunition and medical supplies they were worn down by a constant barrage from the German Army who were keen to kill the group of men before continuing their counter-attack against the rest of the invading force.

Desperate and cut off from help, the men decided to release William with a message informing headquarters of the situation, warn of the impending counter-attack and request air support. However, William was trained to return to Knutsford not the divisional head quarters at Renkum Heath. This would no doubt add flying time to the journey and this was a luxury the men did not have. Nevertheless, they had to make contact with other battalions to find out what the situation was and communicate that they were in danger and should retreat.

It was decided that at nightfall two men would sneak to a clearing in the woodland to a bridge and William would be released with an SOS message. At 22:30 hrs on 19 September 1944, the two soldiers crept out from their defensive position with William in a small cage, they were not seen or heard by the German troops who were still firing into the darkness. When the two men reached the bridge they attached the message to William's leg and tried to throw him up in the air, but he simply refused to fly off and sat perched on the bridge, unaware of the danger or urgency of the situation. A remarkable scene ensued with the two soldiers attempting to 'shoo' William off into the air in mid-battle, he still refused to go until finally the men decided to fire a Sten gun into the air to scare him off.

Once away, William needed no encouragement and completed the journey to his loft in England, a distance of 260 miles, in four hours twenty-five minutes at an average speed of 61 mph. This is a remarkable achievement and William covered 1,740 yards each minute in conditions that were not favourable. Sadly, the message arrived too late for reinforcements to be organised and the men of 2 Para were killed or captured in a final push by the Panzer Divisions who later praised the fighting spirit and resilience of Major Frost's men. However, with the news from William and the capture of 2 Para a full-scale withdrawal was ordered; Operation Market Garden had failed. After nine days of fighting the men from the depleted Airborne division were withdrawn in Operation Berlin thanks, in part, to the efforts of William's intelligence. Total Allied casualties reached 13,000 men and the German army captured 6,000 men whilst just 2,000 withdrew from the area with their lives. Arnhem remained in German hands until April 1945.

Paratroopers were ill-equipped for the boggy conditions underfoot and the water ditches made the attempt to reach 2 Para very difficult. Intelligence reports from the well-organised Dutch resistance were not used and progress along Hell's Highway was tortuous as anti-tank guns bombarded the paratroopers and tanks as they moved toward Arnhem. During the nine days, fifty new tanks reinforced the SS Panzer resistance, the paratroopers had no answer to this firepower.

William was awarded the Dickin Medal for delivering the message in excellent time, which led to the safe rescue of up to 1,000 men in the swift withdrawal. At the end of the war William's owner, Sir William Proctor Smith, bought him out of service for £135, quite a sum in those days and he enjoyed a long retirement. It was recorded that ten years later he was still alive although too old to race or breed.

Ricky
Holland, 1944

It is no exaggeration. We were within 3 feet of the mine in the middle of a minefield. I am confident he was as steady as the Rock of Gibraltar and I think it was his coolness that brought us out of a sticky patch safely.

Ricky was a tousle-haired Welsh Sheepdog bought for 7s 6d by a Mrs Lichfield in Bromley, Kent when he was four months old. When the call for animals was made by the War Office, Mrs Lichfield volunteered Ricky and he was trained to detect mines under the watchful eye of his handler, Mr Maurice Yelding. On 3 December 1944, the German Army was retreating across Europe and set about placing booby traps and laying minefields to delay the advancing allies. Ricky was assigned to detect mines along the verges of canal banks in Nederweent, Holland, which would then be cleared by troops. During this operation the section commander was killed by a mine as troops moved through the verges. The explosion also injured Ricky, who was just 3 feet away, he suffered wounds to his head and damage to his hearing. It is the actions of Ricky at this time that won him the Dickin Medal as he remained calm and continued to do his work detecting mines, despite his injuries. The impact Ricky's composure had on the troops around him cannot be underestimated as they had lost their commander and were conducting extremely dangerous work. If Ricky had become excited he would have been a danger to himself and the men around him, some of whom were working on anti-personnel mines.

The PDSA awarded Ricky his medal in May 1947 by Air-Chief Marshal Sir Frederick Bowhill and, despite his visible injuries, also had a portrait painted to further reward his bravery. Ricky is special because he saved the lives of the men around him by his reaction to the exploding mine that killed his section commander. Furthermore he continued to complete his work although badly injured and located every mine along the canal, setting an example to those around him.

Mercury
Denmark, 1942

Trained and owned by Mr Catchpole of Ipswich, Mercury was the 38th winner of the Dickin Medal. Many pigeons won this medal by completing many flights through a hail of bullets, bad weather or completing a flight after suffering an injury but Mercury was different.

In July 1942, Mercury (NURP.37.CEN.335), a blue hen, was selected alongside twelve other birds from the Special Section Army Pigeon Service to work for the Danish resistance fighters. The pigeons were smuggled to the underground fighters in Denmark and were to be used to transport information about German military strength and shipping in the country. This method had been used before and the pigeons were selected for their ability to home over long distances. The resistance agents were in the very northern tip of Denmark. After managing to gather intelligence on German shipping, they prepared Mercury and the other eleven birds for the flight. The information was considered so vital that on the morning of 26 July 1942 all twelve birds were released with the same mission – to fly 1,520 miles home to England and return the details safely.

Days passed with nothing seen or heard of the birds. The dangers were considerable on such a long flight as many birds were shot for food, attacked by predators, fell into the sea or simply got lost. It was thought that all of the birds had failed. However, on 30 July, four days after they were released, one bird arrived in England. It was Mercury who appeared in good health with his message intact. At the time this was thought to be one of the most outstanding single performances made by a bird serving with the Special Section Army Pigeon Service. Mercury was the only bird out of the dozen to complete her mission.

Mercury received her medal at the PDSA Chelsea Show on 7 September 1946. The citation on her medal reads:

For carrying out a special task involving a flight of 480 miles from Northern Denmark whilst serving with the Special Section Army Pigeon Service in July 1942.

Bob

North Africa, 1943

Bob was a crossbred Labrador Collie of pure white with jet black ears and forehead. He attended the War Dog's Training School and built up a great friendship with his handler, Company Quartermaster Sergeant Cleggett, before they embarked on duty together in North Africa in 1942. Bob's duties included carrying messages and accompanying patrols into enemy territory with C Company of the 6th Queen's Own Royal West Kent Regiment. Like his infantry comrades, Bob was smothered in camouflage paint for patrols and would lead the excursions, giving a signal when he sensed enemy troops in the vicinity.

In January 1943 at Green Hill in North Africa, Bob joined a patrol as a message carrier. Any vital information the patrol discovered about enemy positions or supply lines would be immediately attached to Bob's collar and he would be sent back to headquarters with the intelligence. As the patrol progressed toward enemy lines, Bob halted and signalled that the enemy were ahead. The patrol leader could not see or hear anything and indicated they would move forward, but Bob was not to be moved. It was clear from the latest intelligence reports that the enemy were not in this area. The patrol stayed silent.

A matter of 10 or 12 yards away an enemy sentry became visible to the men as he moved along the grass with his back towards them. The men silently retreated with vital information about the whereabouts of German positions. Bob was a special animal who had a calm temperament remaining silent throughout his missions and providing prior warning of the presence of German troops. Without his intervention, those men at his side would have been captured or even attacked and killed or wounded. Not only that, Bob's intervention secured the vital information about enemy positions. Sergeant Cleggett said:

I don't think any dog has ever been under such a barrage of guns as he has and not one blink of an eye. Believe me, he is a dog of the ages.

Bob was given a regimental battle dress from the men whose lives he saved with his rank and decoration on the left breast. As the war came to an end, Sergeant Cleggett was demobbed and flew back to Britain, but he warned that Bob would not react well to quarantine or strangers. The Allied Forces Mascot Club paid for Bob to be brought back to Britain from Italy and Bob was taken to a train station in Milan. It was here that he broke from his collar and ran away from the bustling station platform. The men who were transporting him searched the surrounding area in vain; Bob had vanished.

The War Office and the Allied Forces Club tried to trace him and his description was broadcast throughout Italy but he was never found. For three years Bob and his handler had been inseparable and his disappearance saddened many. Bob's Dickin Medal was awarded, in his absence, to his owner in 1947. Bob's citation reads:

This is to certify that Bob has been awarded the Dickin Medal for Gallantry, for constant devotion to duty with special mention of patrol work at Green Hill, North Africa while serving with the 6th Queens Own Royal West Kent Regiment.

Maquis
France, 1943–44

After the German occupation of France in 1940 many men and women left their homes and families, refusing to live under foreign rule; preferring to hide out in the mountains. Gradually they became organised and began a campaign of sabotage against the enemy by destroying railroads, airfields and barracks. These groups were named after a bush that grew high up in the mountains in which they hid called 'Maquis'. The missions the groups undertook were fraught with danger and many lost their lives. The German forces would take out their frustration on the inhabitants of local towns and villages when the Maquis enjoyed success.

NPS.43.36392 was a blue chequered cock pigeon bred in 1942 by the Brown brothers in Gratton Road, Bedford. The bird was renowned for his reliability and it was this quality that earned him the most important missions working for combined operations.

The first mission was in May 1943. He was sent with a British agent by parachute into Amiens and returned four days later un-injured and with a message strapped to his leg. He completed a similar mission the following year, returning with an operational instruction. In February 1944 he accompanied Combined Operations into enemy occupied France and was dispatched with a message and arrived at his loft in London the same day, again with the message intact and no injuries. Finally NPS.43.36392 was used in the D-Day landings and returned within a day to his loft with details of the successful invasion. After this flight and his rugged determination and bravery he was named Maquis after the men and women fighting for their freedom. Maquis' citation reads:

For bringing important messages three times from enemy occupied country, viz: May 1943 (Amiens) February, 1944 (Combined Operations) and in June, 1944 (French Maquis) while serving with the Special Service from the continent.

Maquis was demobbed and sold for £22. His new owner, Mr P. Cope from Duxford, used him for breeding and Maquis went on to father what was described as 'the perfect pigeon'. He was awarded the Dickin Medal in October 1945.

Judy

China, Ceylon, Java, England, Egypt, Burma, Singapore, Malaya, Sumatra and E Africa, 1942–45

At the notoriously brutal Medang prisoner of war camp during the summer of 1942 British and Australian prisoners of war worked on constructing a railway line through the Sumatran jungle. Each man was given a meagre portion of rice, barely a handful, as a daily ration. Airman Frank Williams was starving and painfully thin after working all day in the sweltering heat when Judy, a pedigree pointer bitch, came and sat on the floor of the hut near his feet. Frank shared his rice with Judy and from that moment they were inseparable.

Born in Shanghai in 1936, Judy was originally a mascot for HMS *Grasshopper* during the war in the Far East but in February 1942 the ship was destroyed in a bombing raid just off the coast of Sumatra, Indonesia. Some of the crew, along with Judy, managed to swim to a small deserted tropical island. There was no fresh water on the island and death from thirst appeared inevitable until Judy was seen with her nose buried between two rocks; she had found a fresh water spring that had been hidden by the high tide. The crew survived until they were picked up by a Chinese boat and they, with Judy, were taken to Sumatra where they decided to cross the island on foot to reach Padang, a free city at the time. On 10 March as they neared their destination they were surrounded by Japanese troops and all the men, including Judy, were taken to Medan in the northern part of Japan.

Life was hard for the prisoners as they were instructed to build bridges, lay railway track, and even dismantle an old Ford car works in Medan. Many died through exhaustion and each man was given the same rations for a day of slave labour; ten cents per day and rations of two meals per day consisting of watery rice or 'pap', a thin leaf soup or a mysterious mess called 'ongle-ongle'. Every scrap was vital, if a man was sick or unable to work they were denied pay and food making a difficult situation worse; needing nourishment to regain health the man was further weakened by starvation.

Frank began to eat his daily ration of pap and looked at Judy who was sat next to him, he offered her some of the rice but she refused to take it. Frank tried again; he placed some on the floor next to her and patted her head. Judy then ate the small amount Frank could spare. Frank began to look after Judy, always sharing his rations with her and persuading the brutal guards in the camp not to kill her, although it often meant he was beaten up instead. In return Judy would patrol the hut and give warning if poisonous snakes or scorpions came near and retrieving fruit which, in the place of flowers, was laid on graves. She also lifted the spirits of the men and many would say that if Judy could hang on and make the best of it then they would too. Judy would roam the jungle near the camp to forage for extra food too, on one occasion she found the shin bone of an elephant and dragged it back to camp. The men had an enjoyable evening's entertainment watching Judy as she carefully selected a place to bury it then took two hours to dig a hole big enough. If danger approached Frank would shout, 'Scramble!' and Judy would disappear into the undergrowth. She was lucky to survive these forays into the jungle as wild dogs were shot for food and the feared Sumantran Tiger had been seen near the camp, Judy even chased an alligator and nearly lost her left eye when she caught up with it.

Judy would often return with a snake or creature that the men could share and on one occasion even returned with a human skull. It was not from a POW but an old Malayan skeleton and viewed as a bad omen by the Japanese guards. As she dashed through the camp to show Frank her latest 'find', the guards approached to hit her but they soon ran away when they saw what she was holding in her mouth. Judy produced a family of nine pups too, news of which spread to the nearby Dutch women's camp via local fruit pickers who were permitted to sell their goods in the camps. The women sent a message to request a puppy. Frank was happy to oblige but it would be near impossible to get the animal past the guards who stringently checked everything going in and out of the camp. Nevertheless, an attempt was made; chloroform was stolen from the camp surgery and a puppy, Sheikje, was anaesthetised, wrapped in cloth, placed at the bottom of a large basket and covered with bananas. The fruit pickers were bribed to take the 'cargo' to the Dutch camp. The guards did not suspect and the women were delighted to have their own camp mascot. The other pups were great morale boosters for the prisoners; Rokok was given away to a Swiss Red Cross official in

Medan, Punch survived in the camp but Blackie, a bundle of cuddly black fur, was beaten to death by a drunk Korean guard.

Despite surviving these challenges a greater test surfaced. Frank and the other prisoners were to be transported to a new camp so they could work on a different stretch of railway – Judy was to remain behind. The camp commandant, Colonel Banno, sympathised with Frank and showed some affection for Judy; he had a local lady friend who would visit him at work and, as she passed through the camp she would call, 'Judy, come', and pat her. As Judy had recently had the litter courtesy of a foray into the jungle, Frank seized his chance and decided to offer one of the puppies to Banno for his friend in exchange for registering Judy as an official prisoner of war. It was a huge risk, any prisoner who had the affront to talk to a Japanese officer was likely to face immediate execution. Nevertheless, Frank waited until Banno was known to be drinking alone in his hut and was shown in by guards with a pup named 'Kish', which he placed on the desk. The colonel roared with laughter when Kish waddled across the desk to lick his hand; Frank explained why he had brought the puppy and Banno was delighted.

Banno explained that he could not register Judy as his superiors would start asking questions about why there was an additional number on the list of prisoners. Frank foresaw this problem and suggested that if Banno could add the letter 'A' to his own number (81 Medan) Judy could have her own number and simply not appear on the official list. Banno, holding Kish as the pup licked his hand, agreed and took out some paper from his drawer and made the request official. Unaware of the situation, Kish produced a large puddle next to the Colonel's elbow as he scribbled out the order to his guards, Frank seized the precious paper and made his way quickly to his hut. The next morning Judy became prisoner number 81A in Medan, she was the only animal ever to be a registered POW even having her own tag with her new number on.

Unfortunately this was not enough; Banno was replaced shortly afterwards by a new commandant named Captain Nissi. From the first day of his arrival the prisoners knew things were going to get much worse; his first action was to have every man out in the compound so he could see them and when he said every man, he meant it. Those that could not stand were supported by others who could;

the sick and dying were laid out in a long row as he strutted up and down striking his leather boots with his cane. Nissi then stopped dead, staring in disbelief; a dog in a prison camp. And not just a dog, but a prisoner's dog. Nissi marched toward Frank who quickly thrust his hand into his pocket and fished out the vital piece of paper signed by Colonel Banno. Nissi snatched it from his hand and started an animated discussion with the guards. Frank knew if Nissi gave an order for Judy to be killed it would have to be carried out, otherwise Nissi would lose face. Thankfully, after five minutes of heated debate Nissi thrust the piece of paper back at Frank and walked off; Judy was safe, for the time being.

Judy still had to remain in Medan whilst Frank would travel to another camp. Frank would not give up and decided he was going to take Judy with him. It would not be easy, the men were to be taken to Singapore, which meant a long journey over land and sea, the guards knew an attempt to smuggle Judy would be made and remained on red alert. Frank decided he would train Judy to jump in and out of a sack and carry her when they were heavily guarded then rely on Judy's strict obedience and her understanding of his signals to evade capture. Frank and Judy spent hours preparing and Judy had become fully involved in the game; she was excellent and when Frank clicked his fingers (the signal) she would disappear into the sack like a flash. Frank tied Judy to a stake in the undergrowth, but made sure the knot was loose enough for her escape when he called her. Nissi then had all the men stand in the compound again in the searing midday heat for two hours whilst they searched the camp to find Judy. Frank had a large sack on his back filled with blankets, this was the first thing to be searched. When Nissi was satisfied, the men began their trek away from Medan.

As they moved away Frank called for Judy and she appeared from the jungle and, positioning herself between the men as they walked toward the port, Judy managed to get into the port unnoticed. Hundreds of prisoners gathered on the dock waiting to move up the gangplank of the SS *Van Waerwijck*. Judy pressed hard against Frank's legs and he realised now was the time for the sack trick. He opened the sack as a group of men huddled around him and Judy jumped in, Frank then hauled it onto his shoulders and joined the queue to board. Judy was a heavy dog and the ropes dug into his bony shoulders, but as he neared the ship Frank thought they had done it. However, out of nowhere Captain Nissi appeared and stood in front of Frank, sneering.

Nissi spoke, 'Ino Murrasini noka?' Frank knew enough to understand these words, 'Dog not come?' Frank suppressed his look of terror and shook his head, Nissi smirked and marched away not realising Judy was curled up in the sack less than a metre from him. Frank quickly marched up the gangplank between two guards with the sack still tied to his back; still Judy did not make a sound. When Frank got below deck he found a small room and opened the sack, Judy was at last released, stiff and hungry but otherwise fine. But this was not the end of her dangerous journey.

The following day, whilst at sea, the SS *Van Waerwijck* was struck by a torpedo. The damage was severe and a fire broke out as the ship began to sink. Frank found himself stuck below deck in pitch darkness with no escape, he called out and Judy came to him, pressing her wet nose against him. The ship began to keel to one side; Frank found a port hole and decided to push Judy through to safety. As he began to force Judy through the whole Frank recalled:

I shall never forget the expression on her face before she fell into the water, as if to say, 'What is all this in aid of?'

Frank saw Judy swim away from the sinking ship and turned back towards the heat and darkness to search for a way out. Along with his friends, Corporal Oakley, Laurie Symes and Bob Soames, he found an escape hatch. As the water rose to their waists they forced open the hatch and scrambled through into dazzling sunlight. The men then leaped from the ship into the safety of the sea below.

Frank trod water and looked for Judy but he could not find her. Fearing she had drowned or attempted to get back onto the ship to save him, he assumed she was dead. Frank and the other survivors remained in the sea clinging to wreckage, they were picked up after two hours and herded onto a Japanese tanker. Frank, covered in oil, was weak and heartbroken. But Judy was not dead. A fellow prisoner, Les Searle, had seen her swimming for the shore with a man alongside her, one of his arms flung across her back. Judy was rescuing survivors from the sea. Time after time Judy turned away from the shore to help men struggling to get to the beach. Finally, she was lifted, exhausted, from the sea by prisoners and hidden under blankets next to the bodies of two Korean guards who had been killed in the blast. Japanese guards from Medan came to pick up survivors and Les Searle lifted Judy onto a truck. As he did so a scream of rage filled the air. Captain Nissi had seen Judy and filled with anger he barked an order, two guards ran toward Les then pointed their rifles at Judy. A second order was then given, finally it seemed the end had been reached. However, the guards, upon hearing the second command, put their rifles by their sides and moved away. The voice was from Colonel Banno. He made it very clear to Nissi that Judy was not to be harmed and she was taken back to Medan.

After food and some rest Judy recovered and immediately began her search for Frank; time after time, in and out of huts she went but Frank was not to be found. Judy sat near the entrance to the camp watching the trucks as they brought prisoners back from the shipwreck. After two days of waiting, still no Frank. However, Judy remained at her post. On the third day another truck returned and stopped in the compound square allowing the 'walking skeletons' to get out. One was struck from behind by a guard for moving too slowly and he crumpled to the floor. Before the man could turn around he was jumped on by Judy, who licked his face and barked wildly; it was Frank. The two were together again.

In the next few months of 1944, Frank and Judy moved from camp to camp, surviving as best they could. Frank would always carry with him the piece of paper from Colonel Banno that proved Judy was a prisoner of war and she remained unharmed. Eventually they reached a camp run by Captain Nissi, who, upon catching sight of Judy alive and well flew into a rage. Without Colonel Banno present to save Judy she was condemned to death and the prisoners would eat her for dinner as an extra punishment. Frank whispered, 'Scramble!', and Judy ran off into the jungle. Nissi sent men to catch her but Judy outran them. The war was reaching its end and Frank realised that if they could hide Judy for a short while, she may survive. Judy became a 'ghost dog', appearing only on the call of Frank and spending most of her time in the undergrowth evading capture.

The camp was liberated by British forces in 1945, who were appalled at the condition of the prisoners, Frank and Judy had survived. They were taken to Singapore and remained for one month whilst they recovered their strength, Frank then received a place on the ship *Antenor* bound for Liverpool. Wishing to take Judy home to England Frank was dismayed to read the rules, which included 'no dogs'. Frank was not put off so easily; Judy had been smuggled aboard a Japanese ship, why not a British one? This time though it was much easier. Frank waited for a quiet spell near the gangway and arranged for four friends to walk up into the ship engaged in loud conversation. Frank then whistled for Judy, who was hiding between kitbags on a luggage trolley, and she slipped quietly up the gangway and onboard. Frank revealed Judy to a few trusted men and they all helped out, including one of the chefs in the galley who provided Judy with her own meals.

On arrival in Liverpool, Judy was taken into quarantine for six months. Not even Frank could evade this law. Judy looked bewildered as she was taken away from Liverpool docks to Hackbridge Quarantine Kennels but Frank visited her regularly and the six months passed quickly. Whilst away Judy had become a celebrity. The PDSA had heard of her exploits through a recommendation for the Dickin Medal and upon reading her story Judy was immediately awarded the Animal Victoria Cross. The *Daily Mirror* published an article under the headline 'Gunboat Judy Saves Lives – Wins Dickin Medal and Life Pension'. The story of Judy made her famous and she was enlisted as a member of the Returned Prisoners of War Association in London. She was the only dog member. The Tailwaggers Club presented Frank with a cheque so Judy could live out her retirement in luxury.

When Judy finished her six months in quarantine she came out to a reception of flashing camera bulbs, a mass of reporters and cheering crowds. Judy appeared on the BBC Radio's *In Town Tonight* programme. When introduced to the audience she barked loudly at the microphone and became the only dog to 'bark' on BBC Radio. Frank took Judy to children's hospitals and fundraising events, with her medal attached to her collar. Everyone wanted to catch a glimpse of the war hero. The citation on her Dickin Medal read:

For magnificent courage and endurance in Japanese prison camps which helped to maintain morale among her fellow prisoners, and also for saving many lives through her intelligence and watchfulness.

For helping Judy survive the war and his kindness to the animal, Airman Frank Williams was awarded the White Cross of St Giles by the PDSA. After the PDSA was founded in 1917 the St Giles Medal was awarded for bravery when saving an animal from danger or even death, a medal Frank earned many times over.

After Frank was demobbed, he took Judy home with him to Portsmouth. For two years Judy enjoyed life in the seaside town and was often recognised, Frank would take her to his local, the Stamshaw Hotel, and recall her adventures during the war but he would rarely discuss his own experiences. In 1948 Frank grew restless and accepted a position in East Africa with the Overseas Food Corporation to work on the Groundnut scheme to cultivate large areas of Tanganyika with peanuts. He intended to take Judy with him but officials insisted Judy enter quarantine. Frank contacted the PDSA who discovered that the scheme was organised by Lever Brothers and made a request of Lord Leverhulme, as soon as he heard of Frank's problems Judy was given immunity and travelled with him to Tanzania.

Judy enjoyed life in East Africa and had her third and final litter. She enjoyed going on safari and meeting different animals with the exception of the baboons that danced around her and made it impossible for her to decide which to chase first. On one occasion Frank's house boy, Abdul, had dragged a tin bath out of the hut, after Frank had bathed, to be emptied the following day. In the middle of the night Frank and Judy were disturbed by a loud slurping noise, Judy immediately shot outside to investigate and began barking ferociously at a large elephant that had drunk all the bath water. Frank waved his arms and shouted, the elephant skulked away with its thirst satisfied but Judy was not finished. She grabbed the tin bath and began to drag it into the hut despite the protests of Frank, once inside she went back out to bark defiantly at the elephant then curled up in the hut doorway guarding the bath.

In the course of his work Frank moved around East Africa and always took Judy with him. On one flight to Tanzania Judy was required to go into an onboard kennel at the rear of the plane. Usually this would be met with fierce resistance but Judy happily wandered into the kennel and sat down, Frank returned to his seat. When the flight touched down Frank realised why Judy was so content, the kennel had a hole at the top through which she could put her head; next to the hole someone had piled a fresh consignment of game, which Judy presumably though was for her because she had eaten it all!

In February 1950 heavy rain caused flash flooding, Frank decided he would work locally and not stray too far from Nachingwea. On the first day he and Judy set off, they would make a camp in the bush near one of the villages. As the Jeep ground to a halt Frank let Judy out and, as she always did, began searching the area for any sign of danger before returning to the Jeep. Frank busied himself with setting up the camp and visiting a few remaining villagers near Nachingwea. On his return Judy was nowhere to be seen. He whistled and called out but she did not come. The camp natives joined Frank in a search, it had been three hours since he last saw Judy and everyone was worried. One native, Abdullah, found Judy's prints in the dust and began to track her, with Frank following. Abdullah pointed at signs of Judy passing but then, fearfully, noticed the paw prints of a leopard. For two miles along a narrow track, leading to the village of Chumawalla, they tracked Judy but when they reached the village no-one had seen her. Frank sent messengers to local villages offering a reward of 500 shillings for Judy's safe return, but three days passed and there was still no news. On the fourth day, in the afternoon, a native ran into the camp and told Abdullah Judy had been found, alive, in Chumawalla.

Frank, Abdullah and the native jumped into his Jeep and sped to Chumawalla. A village elder led them to a hut and opened the door. Judy was in a bad way; she struggled to her feet, meekly wagged her tail and collapsed. The men wrapped her in blankets and drove back to their camp where they began to treat Judy, removing hundreds of cattle ticks from her coat, bathing her and dabbing her cuts with disinfectant. Judy then ate some food and fell asleep. As the days passed Judy gained more strength but on the evening of 16 February she began to cry. Frank sat with her through the night, but each time Judy woke, she cried. In the morning she could not stand and Frank carried Judy, still crying, through the village streets to the Nachingwea hospital. An Englishman, Doctor Jenkins diagnosed a mammary tumour and operated immediately, it was a success. But within a few hours Judy was in great pain from a tetanus infection.

116

Despite fighting all her life, this battle was too great. Dr Jenkins said, 'Let me end it, Frank,' Frank nodded and turned away. On 17 February 1950 at 5.00 pm Judy was put to sleep.

Judy was wrapped in the Royal Air Force jacket that she proudly wore at Crufts, placed in a coffin and buried on a hill near Nachingwea, not far from Frank's hut. Frank and some natives spent many long hours in the bush collecting pieces of white marble that were broken down and mixed with concrete and poured over the heavy rocks on Judy's grave. This was polished by hand until it met with Frank's satisfaction. Finally he erected a plaque which read:

In memory of
Judy DM Canine VC
Breed English Pointer
Born Shanghai February 1936, Died February 1950
Wounded 14 February 1942
Bombed and sunk HMS Grasshopper
Lingga Archipelago 14 February 1942.
Torpedoed SS Van Waerwijck
Malacca Strait 26 June 1943.
Japanese prisoner of war March 1942–August 1945
China Ceylon Java England Egypt Burma
Singapore Malaya Sumatra E Africa
They Also Served

As Frank erected the plaque he stood over the grave and spoke quietly, 'To a gallant old girl, a wonderful dog, which, with wagging tail, gave more affection and companionship than she ever received.'

NURP.38.BPC.6

France, 1941

This particular pigeon was not given a name. She was bred by Mr Stan Bryant of 20 Victoria Road in Bridgewater, Somerset and was a chequered hen. Stan was a renowned pigeon fancier and his loft was situated in the backyard of 20 Victoria Road. Stan was highly regarded for his skill in nurturing the best out of his pigeons and he worked as a clock-setter for forty years for the National Flying Club. In national competition his results were excellent.

Stan sent many pigeons on war service but sadly lost twenty. This record was considerable as 16,554 pigeons were used on operations during the war and only 1,842 returned. Stan's most famous pigeon was recruited to ferry messages from Bridgewater to the French Resistance. Prior to this, the bird was awarded a Special Section award for the best operational record.

The bird completed two exceptionally difficult flights from Angers on 10 July 1941 and, later, from Chartres in September 1941. Each time she was dropped in a cage by parachute to the resistance fighters in France. The significance of these flights was immense as contact with the French Resistance was essential to destabilising the Nazi war machine. Each time she returned to her loft in 20 Victoria Road with her message, Stan would pass it on to Mr W. Gratton, the pigeon supply officer.

However, a flight from Montagne, where the French Resistance set her free, was fraught with problems. The appalling weather conditions made flying difficult and navigation impossible. It is not known what happened to this bird but it is thought she perished through exhaustion as many birds did in terrible weather. The instinct to reach home often means pigeons will not stop and wait for the weather to clear. As a result they will fight the weather and continue, thus exhausting themselves and falling to the ground or into the sea.

Stan was serving in the forces when his pigeon was awarded the Dickin Medal and his father, Mr W.J. Bryant, received the medal on his behalf. The inscription reads:

Medal for the best operational record. Returned 10.7.41 Angers; 9.9.41 Chartres; 29.11.41 Montagne. Owner Mr S. Bryant.

This was one of the few posthumous awards and each time the owner collected the medal in recognition of their creature's contribution to the war effort.

PART 6

SECRET ANIMALS

Gustav

Normandy, 1944

Gustav holds a unique position; of all the pigeons who have won the Dickin Medal, he was recognised by the Imperial War Museum as the greatest to have served his country. Gustav (or NPS.42.31066) was a grizzled cock trained by Frederick Jackson from Cosham. Gustav had a 'wife' named Betty, who was also an active member of the Pigeon Service.

Gustav began his career in Belgium working for resistance fighters by relaying secret messages from the continent back to his handler, Sergeant Harry Halsey, in Britain. During this service Gustav built up a reputation for consistency and reliability when returning to his loft with messages; for this he was selected for a most important mission. Prior to the Allied invasion in 1944, Gustav was one of six pigeons in service loaned to a Reuters correspondent aboard an Allied warship. The correspondent, Montague Taylor, was to use the birds to send messages back to mainland Britain to advise how the D-Day landings were progressing. Carried in a wicker basket, Gustav was released on 6 June 1944 near the Normandy coast with the message:

We are just 20 miles or so off the beaches. First assault troops landed 0750 hrs. Signal says no interference from enemy gunfire on beach ... Steaming steadily in formation. Lightnings, typhoons, fortresses crossing since 0545 hrs. No enemy aircraft seen.

Despite being cooped up for long hours Gustav flew 150 miles in difficult conditions with a headwind of 30 mph. The sun, his main navigation tool, was obscured by heavy cloud. Gustav avoided the dangers of German hawks stationed at Calais and made the journey from the Normandy coast to Thorney Island near Portsmouth in five hours and sixteen minutes. This was the first message to reach Britain reporting the success of the D-Day landings. The *Northern Echo* of 7 June 1944 reported how the very first word of the invasion was brought through the exploits of Gustav. For this Gustav won the Dickin Medal for Gallantry, his citation reads:

For delivering the first message from the Normandy beaches from a ship off the beachhead while serving with the RAF on 6 June 1944.

In a life that experienced so much danger dodging bullets and hawks in Belgium and later crossing Normandy, it is unfortunate that Gustav did not live to enjoy a prolonged retirement. Sadly he was killed shortly after the war when trodden on by his breeder whilst his loft was being mucked out.

Scotch Lass
Holland, 1944

Bred by Mr Collins in Mussleburgh, Scotch Lass was given the code NPS.4221610 and trained by the National Pigeon Service at RAF Felixstowe. Her service started at RAF Wick before she was transferred to Felixstowe to prepare for long flights overseas whilst accompanying small naval craft. Birds such as Scotch Lass became very important in the middle part of the war as radio frequencies and codes were being cracked, as was the case with the Enigma machine at Bletchley Park. Pigeons could not be overheard or deciphered.

Scotch Lass enjoyed great success and completed forty-three flights from naval crafts in the North Sea and Holland, demonstrating her resilience and consistency. It was in 1944 that she was selected for the most dangerous work; accompanying an agent into enemy-occupied territory with the mission to fly back to England with essential information. The information in this case was microphotographs.

On 18 September 1944 she was parachuted into Holland with her agent, who was under instructions to take photographs of strategic importance and send them back to England using Scotch Lass. The agent completed the task and attached the film to Scotch Lass with a message and let her go in the early hours. However, almost immediately the bird flew into overhead telegraph wires in the semi-darkness and injured herself badly. The agent rushed to her but, unperturbed, Scotch Lass shook herself and took flight before he could reach her; the agent lost sight of her in the dawn but reported that she was flying haphazardly.

Despite her injuries, Scotch Lass managed to complete the mission of 260 miles, much of which was over water, and arrived at her loft in Felixstowe the same day. For this remarkable achievement and her successful flights for the RAF across the North Sea, Scotch Lass was awarded the Dickin Medal on 31 July 1945 for:

Bringing 38 microphotographs across the North Sea in good time although injured while serving with the RAF in Holland in September 1944.

Commando
Occupied Europe, 1942

In the war years Winston Churchill had a desire to set Europe ablaze using the best men and women to go behind enemy lines on the continent and attack targets. They were called the Special Operations Executive (SOE) and they completed many missions that were deemed 'impossible' by others. When embarking on a mission they selected only the best birds to accompany them and Commando was one such pigeon.

With the code NURP.38.EGU.242 Commando was bred by a Mr Moon in Haywards Heath, Sussex who had himself been seconded into the Air Ministry Pigeon Service and had served in the First World War. With a success rate of one in eight pigeons returning from flights starting in enemy-occupied Europe, Commando was set the task of travelling with the SOE behind enemy lines and being set free with information to fly back to Britain. The remarkable fact about Commando is that he managed to do this three times.

Commando was released in June, August and September 1942 and each time had a metal canister strapped to his leg with vital information on the position of German troops, injured British soldiers and where to collect them, and industrial sites that were used as armaments factories. On each occasion Commando returned, despite the weather being dreadful with heavy cloud and strong winds. Commando's consistency was recognised by the SOE so they only used him when the information was vital or needed to be sent home in great haste. The importance of this work cannot be underestimated as radio operators were shot on sight if caught.

The citation reads:

For successfully delivering messages from agents in occupied France on three occasions: twice under exceptionally adverse conditions, while serving with the NPS in 1942.

Rob (The 'paradog')
North Africa and Italy, 1942–45

One of the most famous winners of the Dickin Medal is the 'para-dog' Collie named Rob who had been bought for five shillings by a farmer named Mr Bayne in Ellesmere, Shropshire, when he was just six weeks old. Mostly black with a white face and a long black bushy tail with a white tip, Rob would become the most decorated animal war hero.

On the farm Rob became a working dog, helping his master gather in pigs and cattle as well as learning to guide the hens out from the garden without chasing after them. For his diligent work Rob was well-fed and allowed to sleep in comfy chairs and lived in the house instead of the barn. In 1941 the Baynes had a son, Basil. Rob showed no jealousy but took it upon himself to look after the child, adding guarding the cot to his list of duties. Rob even helped Basil learn how to walk, by allowing him to cling to his coat as he slowly walked around the farmyard.

During wartime, even on a farm, food was scarce and despite becoming the family pet Mr Bayne felt that Rob would be better off in the care of the armed forces which would be able provide him with more food. Early in 1942 the War Office made an appeal for animals suitable for work to aid the war effort, many were rejected but Rob was quickly accepted and enlisted in the War Dogs Training School at Northaw. With his natural intelligence and calm demeanour he excelled and passed out, in record time, as a patrol dog in record time whilst also showing a talent for liaison exercises. Rob was then despatched, with his handler, to North Africa.

After General Montgomery led the Allies to victory at the Battle of Bizerta a 2nd SAS Unit was formed by Colonel Sir David Stirling and was stationed at Sousse with a considerable supply of ammunition, weapons, food and drink. The quartermaster, Captain Burt, was faced with the steady disappearance of these supplies at the hands of Italian prisoners of war and by Arabs passing through the town. So he decided to enlist the services of a guard dog and requested two from headquarters. Naturally, the SAS only sought the best. One of the dogs was rejected due to ill health but Rob was accepted as he was intelligent, did not bark to demonstrate his pleasure and was utterly fearless; within a few days the pilfering had stopped.

As the weeks passed, Rob became a firm favourite amongst the men, so much so that, later in the war, Sam Redhead, Captain Burt's batman, applied to join the paratroopers simply to be with Rob. One day Rob was smuggled aboard an aircraft by the men and enjoyed the experience. So they borrowed a parachute from an American base who had experimented with the idea of training war dogs to accompany paratroopers into occupied territory. If a dog could be trained to parachute safely they could be a tremendous asset in rounding up the men as they searched to find each other in darkness immediately after a drop, and also as an early warning system should the enemy appear.

The chute was designed to take Rob's weight of 93lbs and his first attempt was from 800 feet. There was uncertainty about how a dog would cope with the demands of such an experience so it was decided a handler would sit with him in the aeroplane, jump out straight afterwards and follow him down. Dogs used by American troops either became so excited they would bark loudly; definitely not the reaction for troops dropping into occupied territory; or could not be persuaded to jump from the aeroplane. As the plane rose from the ground Rob sat contentedly at the men's feet and when his turn came to leap from the plane he bounded out; the rush of air blew his fur on end and when the timed cord 'pulled' he was thrown upwards at terrifying speed but showed no fear. Then he gradually drifted to the ground. Immediately the paratroopers rushed to him and found him sitting quietly with his tongue lolling out waiting to be unhooked from his chute. Rob had passed the first test.

American troops heard about the successful drop and immediately asked for Rob to be transferred to their kennels. The 2nd SAS declined the invitation and placed him on a training regime. Rob completed seventeen practice drops with the objective of performing two roles upon landing; firstly to lie still that so his handler could untie him and, secondly, to round up the men quickly as he used to do with pigs and cattle on the farm in Shropshire. Rob loved it.

Rob accompanied the 2nd SAS on many dangerous missions. On one occasion he was dropped with a party of paratroopers behind enemy lines. He lay still until his handler released him then rounded up the men silently in the pitch darkness. Rob proved invaluable; the men slept soundly during the day with the comfort of knowing Rob would rouse them should danger approach. At night the men would move to the targets and Rob would detect any enemy movements and act as an early warning system. After many months he returned, safely, home to England. Exactly how many missions Rob was part of is unknown but on one excursion behind enemy lines he would prove a hero.

Rob was included on the 'Very Secret List' in the War Office, as a fully qualified 'sky dog' alongside two handlers. As the war progressed the Allies launched an attack on Italy in order to drive toward Germany over land from three points, Russia from the east, the Americans and British from the south and west. Rob joined paratroopers from 2nd SAS in two drops behind enemy lines, however the first drop in July 1943 was a disaster. The situation in Italy was fraught. As the Allies advanced the German and Italian troops reformed lines in the northern part of the country; partisan groups formed and were occasionally hostile towards Allied sabotage missions.

The first drop Rob would join is an astonishing tale. Four teams of the 2nd SAS boarded a cruiser to prepare for a landing at Taranto. Led by Lieutenant McGregor, several men together with Rob moved into German-held Italy to spy on German movements and defence plans for the advancing allies. During this period Rob helped escaping Allied prisoners find safety, while the troops were busy cutting off electricity and telephone lines and destroying bridges and other strategic targets. At night Rob would act as a guard dog and warn the men of any danger. If he saw or sensed the enemy he would silently pace in semi-circles from right to left back and forth. At night he would lick the men's faces to wake them from their sleep. As the group worked their way across country, Rob would relay messages between them over long distances but would only permit his handler to undo the paper from his collar. Some prisoners of war were left to find billets with sympathetic Italian families upon finding that their camps no longer had guards. The vicious SS dedicated a unit to recapture these men. McGregor's team, along with Rob, set about distracting the unit with guerrilla attacks to give the POWs time to escape. Finally their luck ran out and the men became engaged in a firefight with the SS. Only two of the party, one of whom was McGregor, along with Rob, managed to escape to safety four months after they set off on their mission.

After Christmas 1943, Germany had completed the occupation and control of Italy. The Allies began planning the invasion of the country from Africa and chose Anzio. Rob accompanied sabotage teams into the country to prepare for the invasion, on each mission has skill and courage provided the men with great support.

Eventually Rob made it back to his base in North Africa. By this time the Allied war effort had gained the upper hand and preparations were being made to launch the offensive at Arnhem. The 2nd SAS were requested to return to England to prepare and assumed Rob would accompany them. However, Rob was not permitted to gain passage on a Royal Navy ship as dogs were not allowed to travel by boat in wartime; despite the desperate pleas of the SAS no exception was made. Eventually, the captain of a Norwegian freighter took pity on Rob and gave him a berth *en route* to Edinburgh. Once there Rob was immediately placed in quarantine for six months. His two handlers went to fight at Arnhem without him, sadly neither man returned.

In January 1945, Rob's owner, Mr Bayne received a letter from the War Office marked 'Very Secret'. Fearing that Rob may have been killed or injured he opened the letter. Thankfully Rob was safe and well. The letter informed Mr Bayne that Rob was to receive the Dickin Medal for bravery.

The 2nd SAS was disbanded, Rob became the mascot and led the final parade and received the RSPCA red collar and silver medal for valour and Mr and Mrs Bayne were informed that Rob would be demobbed and could return to the farm in Shropshire. Also, as a token of appreciation from the War Office, Rob was to receive a lifetime supply of dog biscuits. As they drove to the train station they wondered how the adventures and wartime stress had affected him. They need not have worried as Rob was soon back to his old self. Immediately Rob began to keep order with the pigs, chase chickens out of the yard and garden and sleep at the foot of the Bayne's son Basil's bedroom door. When chicks escaped from their pen and became caught in long grass and nettles Rob would push his nose into the undergrowth and gently lift them out with his teeth and place them back into their coop. However, he was now dreadful at rounding up cows; instead of moving behind them he would attempt to lead them from the front and looked around expecting them to follow him, as he had done with men from 2nd SAS.

One cold winter night Mr Bayne was awoken by fierce barking from Rob and immediately got dressed and hurried downstairs, Rob was still barking by the front door and when Mr Bayne opened it he bolted out into the darkness. Mr Bayne went after him calling Rob to heel but he disobeyed. When he was found Rob was herding some yearlings that had escaped from their pen. Shortly afterwards Rob did the same again, waking everyone with his barking. This time a valuable cow had stumbled in the barn and her chain was caught around her neck almost strangling her. Mr Bayne managed to use a hacksaw to cut the chain. Without Rob's warning the animal would have died.

Rob had a remarkable life and richly enhanced the lives of those around him, having saved many. It is astonishing that he managed to survive the war having been involved in many dangerous missions where his companions were killed, including two of his handlers. The citation on his medal reads:

War Dog 471/322. Special Air Service. Took part in landings during North African campaign with an Infantry Unit and later served with a Special Air Unit in Italy as patrol and guard on small detachments lying-up in enemy Territory. His presence with these parties saved many of them from discovery and subsequent capture or destruction. Rob made over twenty parachute descents.

In January 1952 the Bayne family realised Rob was struggling with old age and infirmity. His war career, though exciting, had left its mark and he was exhausted. Rob was softly put to sleep and buried on the Bayne farm in Ellesmere. The headstone reads:

To the Dear Memory of Rob, War Dog No. 471/322. Twice VC. Britain's First Parachute Dog who served three-and-a-half years in North Africa and Italy with the 2nd Special Air Service Regiment. Died 18 January 1952 aged twelve-and-a-half years. Erected by Basil and Heather Bayne in Memory of a Faithful Friend and Playmate 1939–1952.

Broad Arrow
France, 1943

The 5th Special Forces Group (Airborne) derives its lineage from two units of Second World War fame – The Office of Strategic Services (OSS) and the First Special Service Force ('The Devils' Brigade'). The OSS was formed in 1941 to collect intelligence and wage secret operations behind enemy lines. Small teams of OSS operatives parachuted behind enemy lines in both Europe and Asia to lead partisans against the Axis Forces. From these guerrilla operations came the nucleus of men and techniques that would form the Special Forces Group.

The Special Forces only selected the best pigeons to represent them. Born in 1941, the pigeon Broad Arrow was trained at the farm of Sir Earnest Debenham in Dorset and was selected to accompany the 5th Special Forces Group on three raids into enemy occupied France in 1943 under the code 41BA2793. Each flight home to London would be followed by a quick return to France via parachute. Communication between the French Resistance and London was important. Details of the success or failings of missions and the organisation of supplies was organised through messages delivered by carrier pigeon. Radio contact was extremely risky for the resistance as German forces had instructions to shoot on sight anyone suspected of radio communication.

Broad Arrow completed the three flights in May, June and August in good time with each message intact. On 29 November 1945 he received the thirty-first Dickin Medal for:

Bringing important messages three times from enemy occupied territory in May, June and August 1943 whilst serving with the Special Forces on the continent.

NURP.43.CC.1418
Normandy, 1944

Attached to the British Airborne Troops, NURP.43.CC.1418 was selected for missions behind enemy lines in France. Teams of men from the Airborne Division would parachute into Normandy, complete the objective and use pigeons to report their success or failure to headquarters in England, before making their way back to Britain.

At the beginning of June 1944, a group of paratroopers dropped into Normandy with this pigeon boxed into a small container. She would remain cooped up for six days until the men had completed their objective and then, on 6 June at 08:37 hrs, she was released with a message. What makes this pigeon special is that she managed to complete the flight in adverse weather conditions with high winds and driving rain, arriving at St Thorney Island at 06:41 hrs on 7 June. This flight was the only one completed in less than a day during the Normandy landings and, given the difficult weather, was a tremendous effort. Sadly, NURP.43.CC.1418 did not survive the war and was listed as missing in action after failing to return from France during a later flight, and was never seen again.

The inscription on the medal reads:

For the fastest flight with message from 6th Airborne Div. Normandy, 7 June, 1944, while serving with APS.

NPS.42.NS.2780 and NPS.42.NS.7524
France, 1942–43

This pigeon, given the code NPS.42.NS.2780 but no name, won the Dickin Medal in October 1945 for bringing important messages three times from enemy occupied country, *viz*: July 1942, August 1942 and April 1943, while serving with the Special Service from the continent.

The bird was housed at the Dorset farm of Sir Earnest Debenham, the founder of Debenhams. Sir Earnest bought Milbourne Wood Farm, a large estate that included some outhouses. These buildings were commandeered by the Army Pigeon Service as they were ideal for pigeons making flights across the English Channel from northern France. The whole operation was, and remains highly classified. None of the locals knew of the existence of pigeons at the farm and the handlers of the birds were not even permitted to read the messages; once a bird arrived the information was immediately handed to a waiting courier who would set off for London.

Signalman William Streeter was employed by the Army Pigeon Service and was stationed at Milbourne Wood Farm. He recalls training secret agents on how to handle pigeons and ensuring that each bird remained in tip-top condition. William was never allowed to see any of the messages and did not even know where the birds were taken to in France. N.P.S.42NS.2780 completed only three flights, the first was from Constance when he was released on 23 July 1942 and returned the same day. The second was from Belgium and the third was from France.

Owned by Lady Mary Manningham-Buller, NPS.42.NS.7524 also completed three flights to earn the Dickin Medal and received the award in October 1945. The first flight was on 23 July 1942, exactly the same day as the first flight from N.P.S.42NS.2780. However this bird was released on 23 July but returned on the 28th. The flight was from Brittany. The second flight was from France, released on 10 May 1943, the bird returned on the 17th. The third flight was also from France and the pigeon returned on 26 July after being released by the agent on the 22nd.

PART 7

WAR IN THE SKY

Kenley Lass
France, 1940

Kenley Lass was a dark-chequered hen pigeon given the code NURP.36.JH.190, and became the thirteenth Dickin Medal winner. After war was declared in September 1939 little happened on the English south coast whilst Hitler turned his attention to Norway. The British government began to drop intelligence agents into France to gain details of German plans and military strength. The problem was how to get the information back to Britain quickly as the German invasion of mainland Britain, Operation Sea Lion, was a real threat.

Kenley Lass was the first pigeon selected to accompany an agent into enemy-occupied France in October 1940 to see if such a bird could reach home to Britain with secret messages. The MI6 agent, code name Philippe, was dropped by parachute with instructions to cover a distance of 9 miles on foot, to avoid detection and gather a variety of intelligence before attaching the details to Kenley Lass for flight back to Britain. The technical difficulties were considered worth the risk. How a pigeon would react to a parachute jump at night whilst contained in a small wooden cage was an unknown. Kenley Lass would also have to be 'stored' until the information could be collected and whilst the agent completed his journey he would be forced to leave her in the care of a member of the French Resistance who had no experience of pigeons. However, after eleven days the details were gathered and prepared for Kenley Lass to take back to Britain. With some apprehension of how she would react, Phillippe released Kenley Lass at 08:20 hrs on 20 October 1940 and she arrived in Shropshire at 3.00 pm on the same day after travelling over 300 miles.

Following this success more pigeons were trained and selected for this type of wartime work and provided sterling service throughout the conflict. On 16 February 1941 a pigeon was required for a similar mission where the bird would be stored for a period before being released. Kenley Lass was immediately thought of and accompanied another agent into France where the agent managed to complete his mission in four days, during which time she remained in a small cage concealed in a house.

It was the success of Kenley Lass that inspired the further use of pigeons, not only accompanying secret agents into enemy-occupied Europe but also on bombers and war ships. Each time a pigeon homed in with a secret message or an SOS distress signal, they followed in the footsteps of Kenley Lass. MI6 was so impressed, pigeons were introduced to the MI9 Service, which was especially created to evacuate secret agents from Europe, and to the Secret Operations Executive when it was formed at the behest of Winston Churchill.

Kenley Lass survived the war and was sold for £3 to Mr Don Cole. Unfortunately Mr Cole could not read or write so no records were kept about her retirement or to what age she lived. The citation on her medal awarded in March 1945 reads:

Awarded for being the first pigeon to be used with success for secret communications from an agent in enemy-occupied France while serving with the NPS in October, 1940.

Mary of Exeter
Occupied Europe, 1940–45

Mary (Nurp.40.WLE.249) served with the National Pigeon Service from 1940 to the end of the Second World War. She was awarded the Dickin Medal for outstanding endurance and displayed breath-taking courage and persistence, not only in her work but also in her recovery from injuries despite the best attempts of the German Luftwaffe to bomb her loft.

Throughout the war a pigeon fancier by the name of Mr Charles Brewer trained carrier pigeons, which he supplied to the police and the army. Mary was one of these pigeons and was used by British agents being dropped into enemy-occupied France. Agents would parachute behind enemy lines with pigeons, in small cages, strapped to their backs. On one of her first missions she returned from occupied France with her message, but badly injured. She had been attacked by a hawk, one of the weapons used by the German High Command to intercept pigeons, and had a gaping wound from her neck down her breast. Mary, however, was nursed back to health and was again soon available for active duty.

Two months later Mary went missing on another mission and three weeks passed with no sign of her return. Then, late one evening, Mary appeared still carrying her message, but with seem-ingly mortal wounds. Mary had been shot by the German army, which often took pot shots at pigeons, partly out of duty to restrict the flow of messages back to Britain, and partly for food. Mary's wing had been damaged and her body contained three pellets. Again, she was nursed back to health but before she could resume duties her loft was bombed.

The German Luftwaffe carried out bombing raids on Exeter and a 1,000lb bomb was dropped near the loft where Mary was housed, destroying houses and other buildings. Many pigeons were killed but Mary again survived and was re-housed in a garage. Two nights later another bomb exploded outside the garage and damaged the loft. Mary escaped from her cage unhurt but was left with a nervous condition.

After a period of recuperation Mary returned to active duty and was sent with an agent to France. Ten days later she was found in a field near Exeter and was soon returned to Mr Brewer who took her to his loft just behind the city walls. Suffering from exhaustion and extremely thin, Mary had a wound running from the top of her head down her neck as well as smaller cuts to her body. Mary was cared for but she was unable to hold her head up without support. Mr Brewer made a leather collar for her, she wore this for a month during which she was fed by hand. When Mr Brewer removed the collar she was able to support her head without assistance.

Mary was retired soon afterwards and in November 1945 was awarded the Dickin Medal for her bravery. Of all the animals to be honoured Mary stands apart for her resilience and willingness to continue to do her duty despite her injuries. It is to animals such as Mary that we owe so much because they repay human care and kindness many times over.

In 1991, to commemorate Mary's achievements, the Lord Mayor of Exeter Margaret Danks unveiled a plaque in her honour near the War Memorial in Northernhay, Exeter. There is also a mosaic in Colwick Street designed by Elaine Goodwin, which commemorates the role of pigeons during the war. Mary has a halo and an encircling inscription mentioning her medal. Mary was laid to rest in grave 351 of the Ilford Animal Cemetery.

Royal Blue
Holland, 1940

Royal Blue was a pigeon that had the distinction of being bred and trained at the royal loft at Sandringham owned by His Majesty King George VI. His name derives from both his royal connections and his breed as he was a blue cock. The king kept a number of lofts at Sandringham and all pigeons were put at the disposal of the National Pigeon Service when war broke out in 1939. Many were very capable birds but Royal Blue stood out for his speed and was drafted into the pigeon service under the code NURP.40.GVIS.453.

From September 1939 with the declaration of war on Germany to the early months of the following year, very little conflict occurred in Europe and the period was known as the 'phoney war'. As 1940 progressed more and more action was seen by the RAF as the Battle of Britain raged in the skies above Britain and the Channel. By October 1940 the war was in full swing and Royal Blue, still less than a year old, was placed in a small cage on board a bomber set for a flight to Holland. The crew was forced to crash-land after coming under enemy fire.

The men released Royal Blue from the cage at 07:20 hrs. They were 120 miles from her loft but she completed the flight in four hours ten minutes. This was the first time a bird had been able to fly back to a loft with details of the whereabouts of a crash-landed bomber. A rescue attempt was launched immediately and the ditched crew was brought safely back to Britain.

In April 1945 the PDSA wrote to King George to ask if he would accept a Dickin Medal on behalf of Royal Blue for:

Being the first pigeon in this war to deliver a message from a forced landed aircraft on the continent while serving with the RAF in October 1940.

King George VI was said to be graciously pleased to accept.

Tommy
Holland, 1945

Tommy (Nurp.41.DHZ.560) was a blue cock pigeon whose remarkable story was entwined with that of a young Dutch national named Mr Dick Drijver. Tommy was bred by a Mr Brockbank of Dalton-in-Furnace from a blue cock and a mealy hen bred by a Mr Jamieson of Renfrewshire. A racing pigeon of some pedigree, Tommy won competitions in Crewe, Stafford and Mangostfield.

When German forces occupied Holland in 1941 they ordered the killing of all Dutch homing pigeons, insisting that the metal ring identifying each pigeon be handed to the authorities. As part of this process Mr Drijver, a young pigeon fancier, had all of his pigeons killed except two he managed to save named 'Tijger' and 'Amsterdammer'. He did this by cutting off their metal rings and switching them with two that were already dead before the German authorities arrived. When his pigeons were killed, the number of birds tallied correctly with the number of rings and did not arouse suspicion. Mr Drijer, armed with Tijger and Amsterdammer, joined the local underground resistance forces and began to train the pigeons at the headquarters in Santpoort. The two birds were used to deliver messages between resistance groups. This worked very well until the headquarters was discovered. Tjiger and Amsterdammer were smuggled to safety but Mr Drijver's cover was blown and he was arrested and placed on a transport train headed for a concentration camp. Mr Drijver managed to jump from the train but, fearful of returning home, went into hiding in Dutch resistance safe houses for the rest of the war. It was during this period that Tommy's path crossed that of Mr Drijver.

During a competition at Christchurch Tommy was released but failed to arrive at his loft due to strong winds taking him off course. Tommy was found in a state of exhaustion in a street in Holland by a young Dutch boy who gave him to a passing postman. The postman knew of Mr Drijver's skill with birds and Tommy was passed on to be cared for.

Tommy was slowly nursed back to health on a diet of water and wheat, but Mr Drijver was not sure that he was well enough to fly. However, on 18 August 1945 the resistance received a message that had to be sent to the British forces immediately. Trijger and Amsterdammer had sadly met an unfortunate end, not at the hands of a German bullet, but when a cat broke into the pen where they were kept and ate both of them. The only hope was Tommy. Despite his weakened state, Tommy was released with a small canister attached to his leg containing a secret message about the existence and location of a munitions factory near Amsterdam. Once released he only flew a few feet in the air and then perched on a windmill with the resistance fighters below frantically trying to 'shoo' him off to avoid detection. Eventually, Tommy set off for England.

Tommy reached Dalton in Cumbria, 400 miles away, the next day but he was badly injured with blood dripping from his breastbone. Mr Brockbank found Tommy and began giving him medical attention when he noticed the canister; the message was intact and immediately handed to the police. Part of the message from the Dutch included a tip-off that if Tommy got through successfully a secret coded welcome message on the BBC Dutch Radio Service News would be broadcast. Two days after Tommy set off, the coded message was heard by Dutch resistance, no doubt welcomed with great celebrations.

Tommy and Mr Drijver both survived the war. Tommy was nursed back to health again and made a complete recovery. Mr Drijver remained in hiding until the Allied Forces liberated Holland. In February 1946 Tommy was awarded the Dickin Medal for:

Delivering a valuable message from Holland to Lancashire under difficult conditions, while serving with the National Pigeon Service in July 1942.

Tommy's award symbolises bravery and determination, not just of the animals who were recognised, but also of the efforts of those in occupied territories who seized every chance to do their bit against the invader. At the presentation Tommy and Mr Drijver were reunited and Tommy received his medal from the head of the Dutch Intelligence Service, Major General Van Oorshot. Mr Drijver, in recognition of his skill and bravery, was presented with two British pedigree pigeons to help him start a new loft. Tommy survived the war and lived out a peaceful retirement until he passed away in 1952, after fathering many excellent racing pigeons.

Duke of Normandy
Normandy, 1944

In the summer of 1940 almost 340,000 servicemen were brought home to Britain from Dunkirk in hundreds of vessels crossing the English Channel; the sea was like a mirror and the weather was sunny. Four years later the D-Day landings were postponed for twenty-four hours due to 30 mph winds and rough seas. June 1944 was one of the wettest and windiest of the century. A group of allied paratroopers from the 21st Army Group landed behind enemy lines in France as part of the D-Day operation and amongst their number was pigeon NURP.41.SBC.219, otherwise known as the Duke of Normandy.

The bird, a grand cock bred in 1941, was concealed in a cage and was taken on the mission with the proviso that he be released once the men could ascertain the success of the D-Day operation. Dropped behind the German beach defences of Normandy, the men were told to make their way toward the Normandy coastline and collect information on the strength of the enemy and the success or failure of the invasion. This information was of the utmost importance for headquarters in London; if the mission was going badly reinforcements could be sent to strengthen the allied attack.

After six days cooped up in his basket, the Duke of Normandy was released with a daunting prospect in front of him. Northerly gales in the Channel and heavy rain were compounded by fierce fighting and hails of bullets and bombs. Despite these hazards the Duke was released with news of the success of D-Day at 06:00 hrs and landed at his loft in London after a flight of twenty-six hours and fifty minutes.

The Duke was awarded the Dickin Medal as he was the first bird to arrive with an operational message from troops active in the D-Day landings on 6 June 1944.

Brian
Normandy, 1944

Brian, an Alsatian cross collie, was the forty-eighth winner of the Dickin Medal and became a fully qualified paratrooper. Owned by Mrs Fetch of Loughborough, Brian was offered to the War Office and trained as a patrol dog for the parachute battalion of the 13th Airborne Division. This Division was selected to take part in the Normandy landings on 6 June 1944. Brian was trained as a patrol dog but his intelligence and calm demeanour under pressure convinced the men they could use him in enemy territory. Brian began training to learn to parachute, then after landing he would round up the men silently. This work was extremely important as a large number of paratroopers would drop into wide areas of France. They could not all carry radios and Brian's role was essential in making sure all the men regrouped.

On 6 June, just after midnight, Brian accompanied the men of the 13th Parachute Battalion on Operation Tonga. After parachuting into France the men had three objectives: firstly to secure the drop zone, to secure the territory up to the River Orne and Caen canal, and finally, take control of Ranville, a small town. It was a dangerous mission as some of the land around the town of Ranville was made up of swamps and bogs. The town itself was believed to house large guns which could be used to target the advancing allies. It was vital that the men succeeded.

The drop zone into which the men parachuted covered a large area. Brian rounded up his unit and they arrived at the rendezvous point. When they arrived, they realised that nearly half the men had not reached the rendezvous point. Many had parachuted outside the drop zone after their plane came under enemy fire and was driven off course, others landed in the marshes and some were killed by the enemy.

Despite their depleted number the men decided they could wait no longer and moved on to complete their objectives. With Brian accompanying them the men managed to secure the territory up to the River Orne and Caen Canal but Ranville was well defended. After some fierce fighting the 13th Airborne Division managed to seize the town. Operation Tonga was a success and Brian played a vital role, without his help gathering the men of his unit together after the parachute drop even fewer might have reached the rendez-vous point.

After the successful D-Day landings Brian was required to accompany the battalion to patrol areas to intercept German troops. The work was hard and Brian was used to guard the paratroopers at night and sniff out enemy soldiers across the French countryside. Brian completed his duties with unswerving determination.

Brian was awarded a special collar along with his medal, the inscription reads:

> *This patrol dog was attached to a Parachute Battalion of the 13th Battalion Airborne Division. He landed in Normandy with them and, having done the requisite number of jumps, became a fully-qualified paratrooper.*

Brian survived the war. Completing his service he was safely returned to Mrs Fetch to live out a peaceful retirement in Lough-borough.

Cologne
Cologne, 1942

The bombing of Cologne, in Germany, started in May 1940 but the first calculated bombing raid began in February 1942, with the aim of destroying the morale of the German people, much like the Luftwaffe had attempted to break the morale of Londoners during the Blitz. Operation Millennium involved 1,000 aircraft, sent by Sir Arthur Harris, to destroy the city and prove to the war cabinet that his bombing missions could hurt the enemy and provide price-less propaganda against Hitler's war machine. Cologne was chosen because it was also the headquarters of a military area under the authority of Lieutenant-General Freiherr Roeder von Diersburg, and was the base for the 211th Infantry Regiment and the 26th Artillery Regiment.

On 29 June 1943 another night raid was planned – 608 aircraft set off from Britain. Aboard a Lancaster bomber on the runway at RAF Bottesford sat a crew of seven sergeants: Gates, Cayless, Mooney, Pike, Dolby, Copeland and Hole. Alongside these men was NURP.39.NRS.144. This pigeon had completed over 100 operational bombing missions. He had homed from diverted or forced landed aircraft from varying positions in Great Britain and Europe during both day and night. NURP.39.NRS.144 was an extremely experi-enced pigeon and used to the wartime conditions of members of the Army Pigeon Service. During the actual bombing of the city, the plane carrying NURP.39.NRS.144 lost radio contact. When the Lancaster did not return to RAF Bottesford, it was assumed the plane had been shot down or forced to land.

There was no news of the aircraft or crew for over two weeks and, as is the nature of war, it was feared they had been killed. However, on 16 July NURP.39.NRS.144 returned to the loft at RAF Bottesford in severe distress with a broken breastbone and other injuries. The feathers had re-grown across his breast, which indicated it was a two week old injury, coinciding with the time the plane was lost; but there was no message in the capsule on his leg. It was impossible to start a search for the crew with no information. It was also unclear whether the bird received any medical attention in the two week period he was missing, or if he had suffered alone. Flying or even trying to scour for grain or water to survive for two weeks must have been extremely painful.

For this bird's remarkable feat of homing from Cologne to RAF Bottesford, a distance of approximately 450 miles, with severe injuries including a broken breastbone, he was given the name Cologne and recommended for a Dickin Medal. The inscription on the medal reads:

> For homing from a crashed aircraft over Cologne although seriously wounded, while serving with the RAF in 1943.

Cologne was one of the most prolific pigeons of the war as most birds completed far fewer operational missions. To complete over 100 and home from Cologne with such injuries was an astonishing feat of determination and bravery.

On this occasion his efforts did not lead to the safe rescue of the crew. Sergeants Gates, Cayless, Mooney, Copeland and Hole were killed in the crash whilst Pike and Dolby were captured and became prisoners of war.

Billy
Holland, 1942

Some creatures received the Dickin medals for many acts of bravery but Billy received his medal for one act of gallantry completed in extremely difficult circumstances when a crew of a Handley Page Hampden bomber was at risk. Billy was just eleven months old when he was selected for wartime service with the National Pigeon Service and is one of the youngest winners of the Animal Victoria Cross.

On 18th February 1942 the bomber set off from RAF Addington during bad weather with Captain Robert Kee aboard as pilot. Sergeants Ruttlidge, Baker and Adams completed the crew along with Billy. Their mission was to lay mines off the Frisian Island of Terschelling. The weather was expected to deteriorate as the night wore on. The mine had to be dropped in a precise position near to the island of Terschelling from a height of 400 feet. As the bomber neared the island, searchlights from the ground illuminated the aircraft and it came under fierce gunfire. Captain Kee weaved and pulled hard on the controls to send the bomber high into the night sky to safety.

After passing through cloud cover the crew decided to make a second attempt. As they approached Terschelling, at 800 feet to avoid the guns below, the radiator grills opened to allow the mine to fall, a shell made a direct hit on the port engine. The bomber went into a spin, plummeting toward the sea below. Captain Kee pushed hard on the controls, slowly the bomber responded and groaned upward, but to no avail, they hit the shallow sea and came to rest on a sandy beach. Remarkably, the mine did not explode.

They had crash landed at 5.10 pm in a snow storm; Sergeants Baker and Adams were killed instantly. Captain Kee moved through the wreckage and found Sergeant Ruttlidge who had broken his leg and was delirious. They managed to escape from the wreckage onto the beach and move away from the crash site. Billy, still in his wooden cage, was with them. Despite the adverse weather conditions Captain Kee realised that they, like many others in such a perilous position, had only one hope and decided to release Billy with a message of their location, hoping for rescue.

The distance Billy had to cover was approximately 250miles in a gale-driven snow storm. Given the inexperience of the bird, the traumatic nature of the crash and the weather conditions the survivors did not hold out much hope of Billy making it home. However, Billy arrived at his loft in England at 1.40pm the following day in a state of complete collapse. Despite his tender age and the conditions, Billy did not give up and achieved the impossible, a rescue attempt was immediately launched.

Billy received his medal on 8 September 1945 for:

Delivering a message from a force landed bomber in a state of collapse under exceptionally bad weather conditions, while serving with the RAF in 1942.

Sadly, the information Billy delivered came too late. Minutes after Billy set off Captain Kee saw torches and heard voices growing louder as men moved closer to the beach. The German troops who shot them down were closing in. Sergeant Ruttlidge, with such injuries, could not escape. Captain Kee decided to flee, safe in the knowledge Ruttlidge would be found and cared for by the Germans. Unfortunately he did not get far, the German troops quickly chased after him as he slowly ran down the beach in his flying-boots. Captain Kee and Sergeant Ruttlidge were both captured and became prisoners of war.

All Alone
France, 1943

In 1946 an estimated 40,000 people visited the Victory show at the Royal Horticultural Hall to view those creatures who had contributed to the war effort. News of the pigeons had been kept secret during the war years to prevent the enemy realising just how important they were. Crowds developed around two cages that were larger than the others. One cage held Searchlight Pied who had a remarkable talent. Usually a pigeon will use the sun to home into its loft and this is what made pigeons so useful once they had been smuggled into enemy-occupied territory. Searchlight Pied was trained to conquer this instinct and to carry important dispatches to agents in France guided only by a searchlight. She was carried by aircraft from Britain to a point within 7 miles of the resistance forces or an agent, from here a beam would be activated from the ground and the bird released. Once flying she would ignore the instinct to home into Staines and follow the beam down to the ground. She would not be misled by any decoy lights either because she had been trained to recognise the guiding beam by its volume of light.

This proved a huge advantage for agents in France as they could move all over the country at pre-arranged points, thus avoiding detection, and Searchlight Pied would be able to follow the beam. Naturally, such a special bird was reserved for important missions.

The other was All Alone who had a Dickin Medal pinned to her cage. A blue hen pigeon bred by Mr Paulger in the yard of The Blue Anchor Hotel in Staines, All Alone performed one of the most outstanding flights of the Second World War. Dropped with an agent by parachute into Vienne south of Lyons the pigeon was trained to complete a long haul flight of 481 miles home to Staines. Once the agent had completed his research in August 1943 he attached his message to the capsule around her leg and set her free. Remarkably, All Alone reached her loft less than thirteen hours later, this was regarded as the best performance by a pigeon in the service at the time. The citation read:

For delivering an important message in one day over a distance of 480 miles while serving with the National Pigeon Service in August 1943.

Selected Bibliography

Books

C. Bishop and A. Warner, *German Campaigns of World War Two* (Aerospace Publishing), 2001.

J. Cooper, *Animals in War* (Corgi Books), 1983.

S.R. Davies, *The Story of RAF Police Dogs* (Private Publication), 1998.

E. De Chene, *Silent Heroes – The Bravery and Devotion of Animals in War* (Souvenir Press), 1994.

R. Doherty, *The British Reconnaissance Corps in World War One* (Osprey), 2007.

W. Finlay and G. Hancock, *Clever and Courageous Dogs* (Kaye and Ward), 1978.

J. Gardiner, *The Animals' in War* (Portrait), 2006.

I. George and R.L. Jones, *Animals at War* (Usbourne), 2006.

E. Gray, *Dogs of War* (Robert Hale Publishing), 1989.

P. Harclerode, *Wings of War – Airborne Warfare* (Weidenfeld and Nicolson), 2005.

A. Harfield, *Pigeon to Packhorse* (Picton Publishing) 1989

A. Hendrie, *The Cinderella Service RAF Coastal Command 1939–1945* (Pen and Sword).

L. James, *The Rise and Fall of the British Empire* (Little, Brown and Company), 1994.

R. Kee, *A Crowd is not Company* (Phoenix Publishing), 2000.

A. Kemp, *The SAS at War 1941–1945* (Penguin), 1991.

J.J. Kramer, *Animal Heroes – Military Mascots and Pets* (Leo Cooper), 1982.

A.Moss, *Animals Were There* (Hutchinson, London), 1946.

J. Newton and Phillip Brandt-George, *The Third Reich – A descent into nightmare* (Caxton), 2004.

P. Nicole and P. Clayton, *Rob the Paradog* (Blue Hill Press, Shropshire), 2008.

Lt Col. A.H. Osman, *Pigeons in Two World Wars* (The Racing Pigeon Publishing Company), 1976.

A. Richardson, *One Man and his Dog – a true story of Antis* (Harrop), 1960.

H. Ross, *Freedom in the Air* (Pen and Sword), 2007.

P. Simons, *Pet Heroes* (Orion Publishing), 1996.

G. Seekamp, *Paddy the Pigeon* (Pixie Books), 2003

D. St Bourne-Hill, *They Also Serve* (Winchester Publishing), 1947.

T. Thacker, *The End of the Third Reich* (Tempus), 2001.

Major-General R.E. Urquhart, *Arnhem* (Pen and Sword), 1958.

E. Varley, *The Judy Story – the Dog with Six Lives* (Souvenir Press), 1973.

Chris Ward and S. Smith, *3 Group Bomber Command – An operational record* (Pen and Sword).

Records
Records of the Allied Forces Mascot Club (Imperial War Museum, London).

PDSA Press Releases

Judy	Roselle
Treo	Salty
Buster	Lucky
Gander	Sadie
Apollo	Simon
Sam	

Magazines
Shropshire Magazine – article by Mrs Bayne
Magazine for Cat Lovers

Websites
Wikipedia
www.historylearningsite.co.uk/palestine_1918_to_1948.htm
www.invaluable.com
www.cdli.newfoundland_gander_hero.hmt
www.bbc.co.uk
www.national-army-museum.ac.uk
www.petplanet.co.uk
www.horseandhound.co.uk
www.50connect.co.uk
www.telegraph.co.uk
www.pdsa.org.uk
www.thisisgloucestershire.co.uk
www.stockportexpress.co.uk
www.rgjmuseum.co.uk
www.pethealthcare.co.uk
www.timesonline.co.uk
www.diggerhistory.info
www.pigeon.org
www.independant.co.uk
www.nationalpigeonday.blogspot.com
www.absoluteastronomy.com
www.216parasigs.org.uk
www.blandfordboys.org.uk
www.thenorthernecho.co.uk
www.news.bbc.co.uk
www.purr-n-fur.rg.uk
www.yourdog.co.uk
www.cdli.ca

BIBLIOGRAPHY

www.invaluable.com
www.pethelathcare.co.uk
www.rgjmuseum.co.uk
www.homepage.ntl.world.com
www.pigeonracingpigeons.com
http://dic.academic.ru
www.blandfordboys.org.uk
www.drchrismorgan.ca
www.rafpa.com
http://cas.awm.gov.au/heraldry
www.dreamdogs.co.uk
www.military-genealogy.forcesreunited.org.uk
www.flyingbombsand rockets.com
www.campbell.army.mil

Newspapers

Palestine Post
Muswell Hill Record
Tooting Gazette
Hampstead and Golders Green Gazette
Bolton Evening News
Widnes Weekly News
Hampshire News
Liverpool Evening Express
Birmingham Mail
The Guardian
Sussex Express and County Herald
Evening Chronicle
Express & Echo
Plymouth Extra
Swindon Evening Advertiser
Bridgewater Mercury, 1/10/40
Somerset County, 5/10/40
Evening Standard, 18/9/46
Ipswich Evening Star, 9/9/46
Evening News, 18/9/46
Western Evening Herald, 29/11/45
Nottingham Evening News, 23/11/46
Newcastle Advertiser, 18/9/45
Ipswich Star, 30/8/45
Belfast Telegraph, 30/8/49

The Scotsman, 4/1/49
Daily Mail
Sunday Chronicle
Sunday Express
Nottingham Journal
Yorkshire Observer
Oxford Mail
The People
Aberdeen Evening Express
Derby Evening Telegraph
The Times
Horse and Hound
Sunday Pictorial
Egyptian Gazette
Sunday Dispatch
West London Press
Express and Echo
New York Herald Tribune
Glasgow Weekly News
Dundee Weekly News
The Rand Daily Mail
South Wales Echo
The Daily Telegraph
East London Advertiser
Middlesex Independent

Other

International Press Cutting Bureau, 19 Grosvenor Place London SW1, extract from
Egyptian Gazette on 31/8/49

American Racing Pigeon Club
Heroes of the Animal World
Picture Post

Thank you to all those who kindly replied to my many letters requesting information and guidance, especially the following;

Lieutenant Commander K.S. Hett, MBE RN
Bob Reeves Snr
Miss Rachel Wells (St James's Palace)
Mrs Nina Buckley

Index